BIG BOOK OF ANIMALS™

General Information

Many of the products used in this pattern book can be purchased from local craft, fabric and variety stores, or from the Annie's Attic Needlecraft Catalog (see Customer Service information on page 47).

Contents

Cuddles Lamb

DESIGN BY SANDRA ABBATE

SKILL LEVEL

EASY

FINISHED SIZE
Approximately 12 inches tall

MATERIALS
- Medium (worsted) weight yarn:
  6 oz/300 yds/170g white
  2 oz/100 yds/56g candy pink
  ¼ oz/12 yds/7g bright pink
- Sizes H/8/5mm and K/10½/6.5mm crochet hooks or sizes needed to obtain gauge
- Tapestry needle
- Sewing needle
- ½ yd 1½-inch-wide pink organza ribbon
- 2 pink ¾-inch ribbon roses with leaves
- 2 black 9mm animal eyes
- Fiberfill
- Sewing thread

GAUGE
With K hook and 2 strands held tog: 4 sc = 1½ inches; 3 sc rnds = 1 inch

PATTERN NOTES
Lamb is worked in continuous rounds. Do not join unless specified; mark beginning of rounds.

Weave in ends as work progresses.

Join with slip stitch as indicated unless otherwise stated.

Chain-3 at beginning of rows counts as first double crochet unless otherwise stated.

INSTRUCTIONS
LAMB
HEAD
Rnd 1 (RS): With size K hook and 2 strands of white held tog, ch 2, 6 sc in 2nd ch from hook. *(6 sc)*

Rnd 2: Sc in each sc around.

Rnd 3: 2 sc in each sc around. *(12 sc)*

Rnd 4: Rep rnd 2.

Rnd 5: [Sc in next sc, 2 sc in next sc] 6 times. *(18 sc)*

Rnd 6: Rep rnd 2.

Rnd 7: 2 sc in each of next 9 sc, sc in each of next 9 sc. (*27 sc*)

Rnds 8–11: Rep rnd 2.

Rnd 12: [Sc in next sc, **sc dec** (*see Stitch Guide*) in next 2 sc] 9 times. (*18 sc*)

Sew eyes to Head between rnds 6 and 7, leaving 2 sc between eyes.

Rnd 13: Rep rnd 2.

Rnd 14: [Sc in next sc, sc dec in next 2 sc] 6 times. (*12 sc*)

Stuff with fiberfill.

Rnd 15: [Sc dec in next 2 sc] 6 times, **join** (*see Pattern Notes*) in beg sc. Leaving a 12-inch end for sewing, fasten off. (*6 sc*)

Weave end through sts of rnd 15, pull to close opening and secure.

BODY
Rnd 1 (RS): Starting at neckline with K hook and 2 strands of white, ch 18, join in first ch to form a ring, ch 1, sc in each ch around. (*18 sc*)

Rnd 2: [Sc in each of next 2 sc, 2 sc in next sc] 6 times. (*24 sc*)

Rnds 3–10: Sc in each sc around. At end of rnd 10, join in beg sc. Fasten off.

Fold rnd 10 flat. With 1 strand of white and working in **back lps** (*see Stitch Guide*) only, sew opening closed.

Stuff.

EAR
Make 2.
Row 1 (RS): With size K hook and 2 strands of white, ch 3, sc in 2nd ch from hook, sc in next ch, turn. (*2 sc*)

Row 2: Ch 1, 2 sc in each sc across, turn. (*4 sc*)

Rows 3–6: Ch 1, sc in each sc across, turn.

Row 7: Ch 1, sc dec in first 2 sc, sc dec in next 2 sc. Fasten off. (*2 sc*)

Sew row 7 of each Ear to Head.

ARM
Make 2.
Rnd 1 (RS): Starting at hoof end with size K hook and 2 strands of white, ch 2, 5 sc in 2nd ch from hook. (*5 sc*)

Rnd 2: 2 sc in each sc around. (*10 sc*)

Rnd 3: Sc in each sc around.

Rnds 4–6: Rep rnd 3.

Rnd 7: Sc in each of next 2 sc, [sc dec in next 2 sc] twice, sc in each of next 2 sc, 2 sc in each of next 2 sc. (*10 sc*)

Rnd 8: Rep rnd 7.

Rnds 9–11: Rep rnd 3.

Stuff lightly.

Rnd 12: [Sc dec in next 2 sc] 5 times, join in beg sc. Leaving a 12-inch end for sewing, fasten off. (*5 sc*)

Weave end through sts of rnd 12, pull to close opening and secure.

LEG
Make 2.
Rnd 1 (RS): Starting at hoof end with size K hook and 2 strands of white, ch 2, 6 sc in 2nd ch from hook. (*6 sc*)

Rnd 2: 2 sc in each sc around. (*12 sc*)

Rnds 3–12: Sc in each sc around. At end of rnd 12, join in beg sc. Leaving a 12-inch end for sewing, fasten off.

Stuff lightly.

Fold rnd 12 flat. With 1 strand of white, sew top of each Leg to rem front lps of rnd 10 of Body.

Sew Head and Arms in place.

FLEECE TRIM

Working between rnds 8 and 9 of Head and starting at neck, with size H hook, join 1 strand of white with sc around first sc, ch 4, *sc around next sc, ch 4, rep from * around, join in beg sc. Fasten off.

DRESS

Rnd 1 (RS): With size H hook and 1 strand of candy pink, ch 32, join in first ch to form a ring, ch 1, sc in each ch around, join in beg sc. *(32 sc)*

Rnds 2 & 3: Ch 1, sc in each sc around, join in back lp of beg sc.

Rnd 4: Ch 3 *(see Pattern Notes)*, dc in same lp as joining, working in back lps only, 2 dc in each sc around, join in 3rd ch of beg ch-3. *(64 dc)*

Rnd 5: Ch 1, sc in same ch as joining, ch 2, sc in sp between 2nd and 3rd dc, ch 2, *sc in sp after next 2 dc, ch 2, rep from * around, join in beg sc.

Rnd 6: Sl st in next ch-2 sp, ch 3, dc in same sp, 2 dc in each rem ch-2 sp around, join in 3rd ch of beg ch, turn.

Rnd 7: Ch 1, sc in sp between beg ch-3 and next dc, ch 2, [sc in sp after next 2 dc, ch 2] rep around, join in beg sc.

Rnds 8–13: [Rep rnds 6 and 7 alternately] 3 times.

Rnd 14: Sl st in next ch-2 sp, (sc, ch 3, sc) in same sp, (sc, ch 3, sc) in each rem ch-2 sp around, join in beg sc. Fasten off.

STRAP

Make 2.

With size H hook and 1 strand of pink, ch 15, sc in 2nd ch from hook, sc in each of next 12 chs, 3 sc in last ch, working in unused lps on opposite side of beg ch, sc in each ch across. Fasten off.

FINISHING

Using **straight stitch** *(see Fig. 1)*, with 1 strand bright pink, embroider nose and mouth. Embroider 1 long straight st around each hoof.

Fig. 1
Straight Stitch

Place Dress on Lamb, with candy pink, sew Straps to top back of Dress. Bring Straps to front and overlap front of Dress, sew 1 ribbon rose over each Strap.

Thread tapestry needle with ribbon, pass needle through a st on Head over right Ear, remove needle. Tie ends in a bow. ■

PIGGY Family

DESIGNS BY PEGGY JOHNSON

PATTERN NOTES

Pigs are worked in continuous rounds.

Do not join unless specified; mark beginning
of rounds.

Weave in ends as work progresses.

SKILL LEVEL

EASY

FINISHED SIZE

Mama pig: Approximately 12½ inches
 tall in sitting position
Baby pigs: Approximately 4½ inches long

MATERIALS

- Medium (worsted)
 weight yarn:
  4½ oz/225 yds/127g
   bright pink
  3½ oz/175 yds/99g baby pink
  2 oz/100 yds/56g light tan
  1 oz/50 yds/28g each white and
   medium blue
  ¼ oz/12 yds/7g light blue
  1 yd each brown and red
- Fine (sport) weight yarn: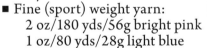
  2 oz/180 yds/56g bright pink
  1 oz/80 yds/28g light blue
- Size 10 crochet cotton:
  1 yd white
- Sizes E/4/3.5mm, F/5/3.75mm and
 G/6/4mm crochet hooks or sizes
 needed to obtain gauge
- Tapestry needle
- Sewing needle
- ½-inch 2-hole dark blue buttons: 2
- Small amount of deep pink felt
- Fiberfill
- Cotton swabs
- Pink lipstick
- Pink sewing thread

GAUGE

Size G hook: 4 sc = 1 inch; 4 sc rnds =
 1 inch

Join with slip stitch as indicated unless otherwise stated.

Chain-2 at beginning of rows counts as first half double crochet unless otherwise stated.

Chain-3 at beginning of rows counts as first double crochet unless otherwise stated.

INSTRUCTIONS
MAMA PIG
HEAD
Rnd 1 (RS): With size G hook and medium weight bright pink, ch 2, 7 sc in 2nd ch from hook. *(7 sc)*

Rnd 2: 2 sc in each sc around. *(14 sc)*

Rnd 3: [2 sc in next sc, sc in next sc] 7 times. *(21 sc)*

Rnd 4: [2 sc in next sc, sc in next st] 10 times, 2 sc in next sc. *(32 sc)*

Rnd 5: Sc in each st around, inc 9 sc evenly sp around. *(41 sc)*

Rnd 6: Sc in each sc around.

Rnds 7–10: Rep rnd 6.

Rnd 11: Sc in each st around, inc 8 sc evenly sp around. *(49 sc)*

Rnds 12–18: Rep rnd 6.

Rnd 19: [Sc in each of next 4 sc, **sc dec** *(see Stitch Guide)* in next 2 sc] 8 times, sc in next sc. *(41 sc)*

NECK
Rnds 20–22: Rep rnd 6. At end of rnd 22, draw up a lp, remove hook, **do not fasten off**.

Stuff Head with fiberfill, stuffing neck area lightly so head can bend.

SNOUT
Rnd 1 (RS): With size F hook and medium weight bright pink, ch 2, 6 sc in 2nd ch from hook. *(6 sc)*

Rnd 2: 2 sc in each sc around. *(12 sc)*

Rnd 3: [Sc in next sc, 2 sc in next sc] 6 times. *(18 sc)*

Rnd 4: [Sc in each of next 2 sc, 2 sc in next sc] 6 times. *(24 sc)*

Rnd 5: Working in **back lps** *(see Stitch Guide)* only, sc in each sc around.

Rnds 6 & 7: Sc in each sc around.

Rnd 8: Working in **front lps** *(see Stitch Guide)* only, sc in each sc around. Leaving a 12-inch end for sewing, fasten off.

Spread rnd 8 outward to be sewn flat to Head when Head is completed.

EDGING
With rnd 8 facing and size G hook, join medium weight bright pink yarn in first unused lp on rnd 4, **ch 2** *(see Pattern Notes)*, hdc in each of next 10 lps, 2 hdc in next lp, hdc in each of next 11 lps, 2 hdc in next lp, **join** *(see Pattern Notes)* in 2nd ch of beg ch-2. Fasten off. *(26 hdc)*

NOSTRIL
Make 2.
Using **lazy daisy stitch** *(see Fig. 1)*, with tapestry needle and brown, embroider sts over rnd 2 of Snout.

Fig. 1
Lazy Daisy Stitch

MOUTH
Using **straight stitch** *(see Fig. 2)*, and referring to pattern (see next page), with tapestry needle and brown, embroider mouth on underside of Snout.

Fig. 2
Straight Stitch

TONGUE

Following pattern, cut tongue from deep pink felt. With sewing needle and thread, fold tongue and sew along dotted line. Sew tongue to underside of rnd 9 of Snout.

Stuff Snout and sew onto rnds 12–19 of Head.

EYES

With white crochet cotton doubled and tapestry needle, sew buttons between rnds 10 and 11 of Head, 1½ inches apart as follows: Working through center top of Head from 1 button to other, sew buttons between rnds 10 and 11, pulling crochet cotton slightly to indent eyes. Sew several times through each eye and to top of Head to secure and indent properly.

EYELID
Make 2.

With size F hook and medium weight blue, ch 7, sc in 2nd ch from hook, sc in each rem ch across. Leaving a 12-inch end for sewing, fasten off.

With tapestry needle, sew 1 Eyelid above each Eye, having Eyelid touch Eye.

EAR
Make 2.

Row 1 (RS): With size F hook and medium weight bright pink and leaving a 12-inch end at beg, ch 8, sc in 2nd ch from hook, sc in each rem ch across, turn. (7 sc)

Rows 2–4: Ch 1, 2 sc in first sc, sc in each rem sc across, turn. (10 sc at end of last row)

Rows 5–10: Sk first sc, sc in each rem sc across, turn. (4 sc at end of last row)

Row 11: Ch 1, [sc dec in next 2 sc] twice, turn. (2 sc)

Row 12: Ch 1, sc dec in 2 sc. Fasten off. (1 sc)

Row 13: Join light tan in end of row 1, ch 1, sc in each row up side of ear, 2 sc in point of row 12, sc in each row down opposite edge of ear, ending in end of row 1 at opposite side. Fasten off.

INNER EARS

Following pattern, cut 2 Inner Ears from deep pink felt. With sewing needle and pink thread, sew Inner Ears to inside of Ears.

With tapestry needle, weave beg end of bright pink on Ear through opposite side of starting ch, pull slightly to curve, knot to secure curve. Sew Ears to Head between rnds 5–8.

BODY

Rnd 1 (RS): With size G hook, pick up dropped lp from rnd 22 of Neck, sc in each st around inc 4 sc evenly sp around. (45 sc)

Rnd 2: Sc in each sc around.

Rnd 3: Sc in each st around, inc 5 sc evenly sp around. (50 sc)

Rnds 4–8: Rep rnd 2.

Rnd 9: Rep rnd 3. (55 sc)

Rnds 10–14: Rep rnd 2.

Rnd 15: Sc in each sc around, inc 6 sc evenly sp around. (61 sc)

Rnds 16–22: Rep rnd 2.

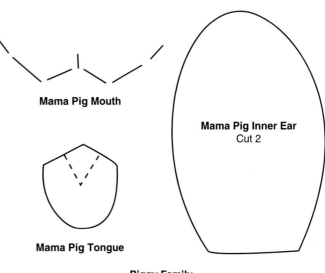

Mama Pig Mouth

Mama Pig Inner Ear
Cut 2

Mama Pig Tongue

Piggy Family
Patterns

Rnd 23: Sc in each st around, dec 7 sc evenly sp around. *(54 sc)*

Rnd 24: Sc in each sc around, join in beg sc. Fasten off.

Stuff firmly.

BODY BOTTOM
Rnd 1 (RS): With size F hook and medium weight bright pink, ch 2, 6 sc in 2nd ch from hook. *(6 sc)*

Rnd 2: 2 sc in each sc around. *(12 sc)*

Rnds 3–9: Sc in each st around, inc 6 sc evenly sp around. *(54 sc at end of last rnd)*

Rnd 10: Sc in each sc around, join in beg sc. Leaving an 18-inch end for sewing, fasten off.

Sew rnd 10 to rnd 24 of Body.

ARM
Make 2.
Rnd 1 (RS): Beg at hoof with size G hook and light tan, ch 2, 6 sc in 2nd ch from hook. *(6 sc)*

Rnd 2: 2 sc in each sc around. *(12 sc)*

Rnd 3: Sc in each st around, inc 6 sc evenly sp around. *(18 sc)*

Rnds 4–6: Sc in each sc around. At end of rnd 6, join in beg sc. Fasten off.

Rnd 7: Join medium weight bright pink in any sc of rnd 6, sc in each sc around. *(18 sc)*

Rnds 8–15: Sc in each sc around.

Row 16: Now working in rows, dc in each of next 7 sc, sc in next sc, turn. *(8 sts)*

Row 17: Ch 2, sk first sc, dc in each of next 6 dc, sc in next dc, sl st in next sc on rnd 15. Leaving a 12-inch end for sewing, fasten off.

Stuff firmly. With dc sts toward back of Body, sew arms ½ inch down from Neck and 4½ inches apart across front.

LEG
Make 2.
Rnd 1 (RS): With size G hook and light tan, ch 2, 7 sc in 2nd ch from hook. *(7 sc)*

Rnd 2: Work 2 sc in each sc around. *(14 sc)*

Rnd 3: Sc in each st around, inc 7 sc evenly sp around. *(21 sc)*

Rnd 4: Sc in each st around, inc 4 sc evenly sp around. *(25 sc)*

Rnds 5–7: Sc in each sc around. At end of rnd 7, join in beg sc, fasten off.

Rnd 8: Join medium weight bright pink yarn, sc in each sc around. *(25 sc)*

Rnds 9–17: Sc in each sc around.

Row 18: Dc in each of next 10 sc, sc in next sc, ch 2, turn. *(11 sc)*

Row 19: Sk first sc, sc in next dc, dc in each of next 8 dc, sc in next dc, join in beg sc. Leaving a 12-inch end for sewing, fasten off.

Stuff firmly. With dc sts at outer sides of Body, sew Legs between rnds 14 and 22 about 5 inches apart across front.

TAIL
Row 1 (RS): With size G hook and medium weight bright pink yarn and leaving a 6-inch end at beg, ch 12, sc in 2nd ch from hook, sc in each rem ch across, turn. *(11 sc)*

Row 2: Ch 1, 3 sc in first sc, 4 sc in each rem sc across. Fasten off.

Sew Tail to Body at center back bottom.

HAT
Rnd 1 (RS): With size F hook and medium weight medium blue, ch 2, 6 sc in 2nd ch from hook. *(6 sc)*

Rnd 2: Sc in each sc around.

Rnd 3: [Sc in next sc, 2 sc in next sc] 3 times. *(9 sc)*

Rnd 4: Rep rnd 2.

Rnd 5: [Sc in each of next 2 sc, 2 sc in next sc] 3 times. *(12 sc)*

Rnd 6: Rep rnd 2.

Rnd 7: [Sc in each of next 3 sc, 2 sc in next sc] 3 times. *(15 sc)*

Rnd 8: Rep rnd 2.

Rnd 9: [Sc in each of next 4 sc, 2 sc in next sc] 3 times. *(18 sc)*

Rnd 10: Rep rnd 2.

Rnd 11: *Sc in next sc, ch 3, rep from * around, join in beg sc. Fasten off.

HAT FLOWER

With size F hook and medium weight baby pink, ch 3, join in first ch to form a ring, [ch 8, sl st in ring] 6 times. Leaving a 12-inch end for sewing, fasten off.

Sew Flower to rnd 1 of Hat. Stuff Hat firmly. Sew rnd 10 of Hat to top of Head.

COLLAR

Row 1 (RS): With size G hook and white, ch 37, sc in 2nd ch from hook, hdc in next ch, [2 dc in next ch, dc in each of next 3 chs] 8 times, hdc in next ch, sc in next ch, turn. *(44 sts)*

Row 2: Ch 1, sc in first sc, hdc in next hdc, [2 dc in next dc, dc in each of next 3 dc] 10 times, hdc in next hdc, sc in next sc. Fasten off. *(54 sts)*

Row 3: With size G hook and light blue, ch 22 *(first tie)*, sl st in opposite side of starting ch, ch 3, sc in end of row 1, ch 3, sc in first sc of row 2, *ch 3, sc in next st on row 2, rep from * across, ch 3, sc in end of row 1, ch 3, sl st in opposite side of starting ch, ch 22 *(2nd tie)*. Fasten off.

Place around neckline. Tie ends at center front.

FINISHING

With lipstick and cotton swab, highlight cheeks as desired.

BABY PIG
Make 4.
SNOUT
Rnd 1 (RS): With size F hook and medium weight baby pink, ch 2, 6 sc in 2nd ch from hook. *(6 sc)*

Rnd 2: 2 sc in each sc around. *(12 sc)*

Rnd 3: Working in **back lps** *(see Stitch Guide)* only, sc in each sc around.

Rnd 4: [2 sc in next sc, sc in each of next 3 sc] 3 times. *(15 sc)*

HEAD
Rnd 5: [2 sc in next sc, sc in next sc] 4 times, place marker at center of increased point to indicate center top of head, sc in each of last 7 sc. *(19 sc)*

Rnd 6: Sc in each sc around.

Rnd 7: [2 sc in next sc, sc in each of next 2 sc] 6 times, 2 sc in next sc. *(26 sc)*

Rnd 8: [2 sc in next sc, sc in each of next 5 sc] 4 times, 2 sc in next sc, sc in next sc. *(31 sc)*

Rnd 9: Sc in each of next 11 sc, 2 sc in next sc, sc in next sc *(center top)*, 2 sc in next sc, sc in each of next 17 sc. *(33 sc)*

BODY
Rnds 10–20: Sc in each sc around. At end of rnd 20, draw up lp, remove hook, **do not fasten off**.

EAR
Make 2.
Rnd 1 (RS): With size F hook and medium weight bright pink yarn, ch 2, 6 sc in 2nd ch from hook. *(6 sc)*

Rnd 2: 2 sc in each of next 2 sc, (dc, ch 2 tightly, sc) in next sc, 2 sc in each of next 2 sc, sc in next sc, join in beg sc. Fasten off.

Sew Ears to Head between rnds 8 and 9, leaving ½-inch sp between Ears.

SNOUT EDGE

With size F hook, join medium weight bright pink in first unused lp of rnd 2 of Snout, ch 1, sc in each unused lp around, inc 2 sc evenly sp around, join in beg sc. Fasten off.

EYES

Using **French knot** (*see Fig. 1*) and working through back opening of Body, with tapestry needle and 12-inch length of light blue, embroider 2 sts ¼ inch apart over rnd 6 of head.

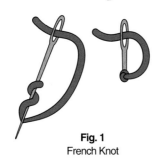

Fig. 1
French Knot

TONGUE

With tapestry needle and 12-inch length of red, form lp at underside of Snout and secure with 2 sts.

Stuff Head and Body; continue to stuff as work progresses.

BODY

Rnd 21: With size F hook, pick up dropped lp of rnd 20, sc in each st around, dec 6 sc evenly sp around. (*27 sc*)

Rnd 22: Sc in each st around, dec 6 sc evenly sp around. (*21 sc*)

Rnd 23: Sc in each st around, dec 5 sc evenly sp around. (*16 sc*)

Rnd 24: Sc in each sc around, dec 7 sc evenly sp around, join in beg sc. Leaving a 12-inch end, fasten off. (*9 sc*)

With tapestry needle, weave end through sc sts of rnd 24, pull tightly and secure.

LEG
Make 4.
Row 1 (RS): With size F hook and light pink, ch 5, sc in 2nd ch from hook, sc in each rem ch across, turn. (*4 sc*)

Rows 2–8: Ch 1, sc in each sc across, turn. At end of row 8, leaving a 12-inch end for sewing, fasten off.

Sew row 8 to opposite side of starting ch, sew 1 end of rows closed.

Stuff firmly. Sew to underside of Body, having front Legs ½ inch apart and back Legs 1 inch apart.

TAIL

With size F hook and medium weight bright pink, ch 12 tightly, sl st in 2nd ch from hook, sl st in each rem ch across. Fasten off.

Sew to back of Body.

PREEMIE PIG

With size E hook and fine weight bright pink, work same as Baby Pig.

PREEMIE BLANKET

Rnd 1 (RS): With size G hook and fine weight light blue, ch 2, 6 sc in 2nd ch from hook. (*6 sc*)

Rnd 2: 2 sc in each sc around. (*12 sc*)

Rnd 3: [Sc in next sc, 2 sc in next sc] 6 times. (*18 sc*)

Rnd 4: [Sc in each of next 2 sc, 2 sc in next sc] 6 times. (*24 sc*)

Rnd 5: [Sc in each of next 3 sc, 2 sc in next sc] 6 times. (*30 sc*)

Rnd 6: [Sc in each of next 4 sc, 2 sc in next sc] 6 times. (*36 sc*)

Rnd 7: [Sc in each of next 5 sc, 2 sc in next sc] 6 times. (*42 sc*)

Rnd 8: Ch 3, *sc in next sc, ch 3, rep from * around, join in first ch of beg ch-3, ch 20 (*tie*). Fasten off. Join fine weight light blue opposite first tie, ch 20 (*tie*). Fasten off.

Tie Blanket around tummy of Preemie Pig. ■

POCKET Pals

DESIGNS BY JANET CHAVARRIA

SKILL LEVEL

EASY

FINISHED SIZES
Approximately 4 inches tall

MATERIALS
- Medium (worsted) weight yarn:
  - 2 oz/100 yds/56g white
  - 1½ oz/75 yds/42g each pastel peach and brown
  - 1 oz/50 yds/28g each scarlet and pale clay
  - ½ oz/25 yds/14g black
  - 2 yds each baby pink, winter white, walnut, light gold and light blue
- Sizes E/4/3.5mm and G/6/4mm crochet hooks or sizes needed to obtain gauge
- Tapestry needle
- Sewing needle
- 3 white 1-inch pompoms
- ½-inch pink pompom
- 13-inch length of ½-inch-wide satin ribbon
- Fiberfill
- White sewing thread

GAUGE
Size G hook: 4 sc = 1 inch; 4 sc rnds = 1 inch

PATTERN NOTES
Pals are worked in continuous rounds. Do not join unless specified; mark beginning of rounds.

Weave in ends as work progresses.

Join with slip stitch as indicated unless otherwise stated.

Chain-2 at beginning of rows counts as first half double crochet unless otherwise stated.

Chain-3 at beginning of rows counts as first double crochet unless otherwise stated.

INSTRUCTIONS
PUPPY
HEAD
Rnd 1 (RS): With size G hook and pastel peach, ch 2, 6 sc in 2nd ch from hook. *(6 sc)*

Rnd 2: 2 sc in each sc around. *(12 sc)*

Rnd 3: [2 sc in each of next 3 sc, sc in each of next 3 sc] twice. *(18 sc)*

Rnd 4: Sc in each sc around.

Rnd 5: [Sc in each of next 2 sc, 2 sc in next st] 6 times. *(24 sc)*

Rnd 6: [Sc in each of next 5 sc, 2 sc in next sc] 4 times. *(28 sc)*

Rnds 7–12: Rep rnd 4.

Stuff firmly with fiberfill.

Rnd 13: *[**Sc dec** (*see Stitch Guide*) in next 2 sc] 3 times, sk next sc, rep from * 3 times. *(12 sc)*

BODY
Rnd 14: [Sc in next sc, 2 sc in each of next 2 sc] 6 times. *(18 sc)*

Rnd 15: Rep rnd 4.

Rnd 16: [Sc in each of next 2 sc, 2 sc in next sc] 6 times. *(24 sc)*

Rnds 17–23: Rep rnd 4.

Rnd 24: Sc in each of next 22 sc, sl st in next sc, ch 1, working in **back lps** (*see Stitch Guide*) only, hdc in same st as last sl st made, hdc in each of next 10 sts, (hdc, sl st) in next st. Leaving a 12-inch end for sewing, fasten off.

Stuff. Press hdc sts flat to form bottom. With tapestry needle, sew hdc sts to opposite sc sts.

LEG
Make 2.
Rnd 1 (RS): With size G hook and pastel peach, ch 2, 6 sc in 2nd ch from hook. *(6 sc)*

Rnd 2: 2 sc in each sc around. *(12 sc)*

Rnds 3–7: Sc in each sc around.

Rnd 8: Sc in each sc around, **join** (*see Pattern Notes*) in beg sc, turn.

Row 10: Ch 1, now working in a row, sk first sl st, sc in each of next 6 sts. Leaving a 12-inch end for sewing, fasten off.

Stuff. With tapestry needle, sew Legs to Body, having row 10 at bottom.

ARM
Make 2.
Rnds 1 & 2: Rep rnds 1 and 2 of Leg.

Rnds 3–7: Sc in each sc around.

Rnd 8: Sc in each sc around, join in beg sc. Leaving a 12-inch end for sewing, fasten off.

Stuff. Fold rnd 8 flat and with tapestry needle, sew across. Sew 1 Arm to each side of Body.

SNOUT
Rnd 1 (RS): With size G hook and pastel peach, ch 2, 4 sc in 2nd ch from hook. *(4 sc)*

Rnd 2: 2 sc in each sc around. *(8 sc)*

Rnd 3: [2 sc in each of next 2 sc, sc in each of next 2 sc] twice. *(12 sc)*

Rnd 4: [2 hdc in next sc, hdc in each of next 5 sc] twice, join in beg hdc. Leaving a 12-inch end for sewing, fasten off. *(14 hdc)*

Stuff. Sew to front of Head.

EYE PATCH
With walnut, ch 2, (3 sc, hdc, 3 dc, hdc, sc) in 2nd ch from hook, join in beg sc. Fasten off.

Sew Eye Patch to RS of Head just above and to left of right eye, opposite position at which left eye will be worked later.

FACE
Using **satin stitch** (*see Fig. 1*), with tapestry needle and black, embroider eyes and nose. Using **straight stitch** (*see Fig. 2*), with tapestry needle and black, embroider mouth as shown in photo.

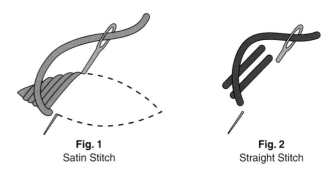

Fig. 1
Satin Stitch

Fig. 2
Straight Stitch

EARS
FIRST EAR
Row 1: With size G hook and walnut, ch 10, sc in 2nd ch from hook, sc in each of next 2 chs, hdc in each of next 4 chs, dc in next ch, 6 dc in last ch, working in unused lps on opposite side of

beg ch, dc in next ch, hdc in each of next 4 chs, sc in each of next 3 chs, ch 1, turn.

Row 2: Sc in each of next 7 sts, hdc in each of next 2 sts, 2 sc in each of next 4 sts, sl st in each of next 9 sts. Fasten off.

2ND EAR
Row 1 (RS): Rep row 1 of First Ear.

Row 2: Sl st in each of next 9 sts, 2 sc in each of next 4 sts, hdc in each of next 2 sts, sc in each of next 7 sts. Fasten off.

Sew Ears to Head with sl st edge of each Ear facing forward.

TAIL
Rnd 1 (RS): With size G hook and pastel peach, ch 2, 4 sc in 2nd ch from hook. (*4 sc*)

Rnd 2: [Sc in next sc, 2 sc in next sc] twice. (*6 sc*)

Rnds 3–5: Sc in each sc around.

Rnd 6: Sc in each of next 2 sc, 2 sc in next sc, sc in each of next 3 sc. (*7 sc*)

Rnd 7: Sc in each of next 3 sc, 2 sc in next sc, sc in each of next 3 sc, join in beg sc. Fasten off. (*8 sc*)

Stuff lightly. Sew to back of Body.

COLLAR
With size G hook and scarlet, ch 24, leaving a 12-inch end. Fasten off.

TAG
With size G hook and light gold, ch 2, 5 sc in 2nd ch from hook, join in beg sc, leaving a 12-inch end. Fasten off.

Loop 1 end of Tag over middle of Collar; secure at back of Tag with a few sts.

Place Collar around neckline; sew ends tog at back.

BEAR
With brown, work same as Puppy through Arm.

SNOUT
Rnd 1 (RS): With size G hook and winter white, ch 2, 6 sc in 2nd ch from hook. (*6 sc*)

Rnd 2: 2 sc in each sc around. (*12 sc*)

Rnd 3: [Sc in each of next 5 sc, 2 sc in next sc] twice. (*14 sc*)

Rnd 4: Sc in each sc around, join in beg sc. Fasten off.

Stuff firmly. Sew to front of Head.

FACE
Work same as Face for Puppy.

EAR
Make 2.
Row 1 (RS): With size G hook and brown, ch 2, 4 sc in 2nd ch from hook, ch 1, turn. (*4 sc*)

Row 2: Sc in first sc, 2 sc in each of next 2 sc, sl st in next sc. Fasten off.

Sew Ears to top of Head.

BOW TIE
TIE
With size E hook and light blue, ch 26. Fasten off.

BOW
Row 1 (RS): With size E hook and light blue, ch 5, sc in 2nd ch from hook, sc in each of next 3 chs, ch 1, turn. (*4 sc*)

Row 2: Ch 1, sc in each sc across, turn.

Row 3: Ch 1, [**sc dec** (*see Stitch Guide*) in next 2 sc] twice, turn. (*2 sc*)

Row 4: Ch 1, sc dec in next 2 sc, ch 1, turn. (*1 sc*)

Row 5: Ch 1, sc in sc, turn.

Row 6: Ch 1, 2 sc in sc, turn. (*2 sc*)

Row 7: Ch 1, 2 sc in each sc across, turn. (*4 sc*)

Row 8: Ch 1, sc in each sc across, turn.

Row 9: Ch 1, sc in each sc across. Fasten off.

Tack Bow to middle of Tie. Place around neckline. Sew ends of Tie tog at back.

DOLL
HEAD

Rnds 1–12: With pale clay, rep rnds 1–12 of Head of Puppy.

Rnd 13: *[Sc dec in next 2 sc] 3 times, sk next sc, rep from * around, join in beg sc. Fasten off.

DRESS TOP

Rnd 14 (RS): With size G hook, join scarlet with sc in same sc as joining, 2 sc in next sc, *sc in next sc, 2 sc in next sc, rep from * around. (18 sc)

Rnd 15: Sc in each sc around.

Rnd 16: [Sc in each of next 2 sc, 2 sc in next sc] 6 times. (24 sc)

Rnd 17: Sc in each sc around.

Rnd 18: Sc in each sc around, join in beg sc. Fasten off.

LOWER BODY

Rnd 19: Working in **back lps** (see Stitch Guide) only, join pale clay in same sc as joining, sc in each sc around. (24 sc)

Rnds 20–23: Sc in each sc around.

Rnd 24: Sc in each of next 22 sc, sl st in next sc, ch 1, working in **back lps** (see Stitch Guide) only, hdc in same st as last sl st made, hdc in each of next 10 sts, (hdc, sl st) in next st. Leaving a 12-inch end for sewing, fasten off.

Stuff. Press hdc sts flat to form bottom. With tapestry needle, sew hdc sts to opposite sc sts.

SKIRT

Rnd 1 (RS): With size G hook, join scarlet in first unused lp on rnd 18, **ch 3** (see Pattern Notes), dc around, inc 16 dc evenly sp around, join in 3rd ch of beg ch-3. (40 dc)

Rnd 2: Ch 2 (see Pattern Notes), hdc in each st around, join in 2nd ch of beg ch-2.

Rnd 3: *Ch 2, dc in same st, sk next st, sl st in next st, rep from * around, join in joining sl st. Fasten off.

LEG

Make 2.

Rnds 1–10: With pale clay, rep rnds 1–10 of Leg of Puppy.

ARM

Make 2.

Rnd 1 (RS): With size G hook and pale clay, ch 2, 5 sc in 2nd ch from hook. (5 sc)

Rnd 2: 2 sc in each sc around. (10 sc)

Rnd 3: Sc in each sc around, join in beg sc. Fasten off.

Rnd 4: Join scarlet in any sc, ch 1, sc in each sc around. (10 sc)

Rnds 5–7: Sc in each sc around.

Rnd 8: Sc in each sc around, join in beg sc. Fasten off.

Stuff lightly. Sew Arms to Body.

FACE

Using **satin stitch** (see Fig. 1), with tapestry needle and with pale clay, embroider several sts in center of face for nose, as shown in photo.

Using satin stitch, with tapestry needle and black, embroider sts for eyes, as shown in photo.

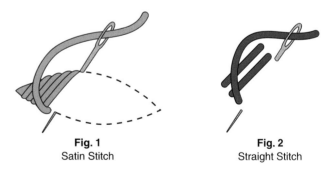

Fig. 1
Satin Stitch

Fig. 2
Straight Stitch

Using **straight stitch** (see Fig. 2), with tapestry needle and scarlet, embroider sts in V-shape for mouth, as shown in photo.

HAIR

With tapestry needle and black, make a series of 7 or 8 lps across rnd 2 at top of Head for bangs.

Cut 40 strands of black, each 10 inches long. Place 2 at a time across head. With tapestry needle and separate strand of black, **backstitch** *(see Fig. 3)* down a center part line, securing strands to Head.

Fig. 3
Backstitch

Bring strands to sides of Head. Tie a strand of black around strands to make ponytail at each side of Head. Tack hair to side of Head. Tie a length of scarlet around each ponytail; tie ends in a bow.

COLLAR

With size G hook and scarlet, ch 23, dc in 3rd ch from hook, *sk next ch, sl st in next ch, ch 2, dc in same ch, rep from * around, sl st in same ch as last dc. Fasten off.

Sew Collar around neckline.

BUNNY

With white, work same as Puppy through Arm.

INNER EAR
Make 2.
Row 1 (RS): With size G hook and baby pink, ch 12, sc in 2nd ch from hook, sc in each of next 2 chs, hdc in each of next 4 chs, dc in each of next 3 chs, 5 dc in last ch, working in unused lps on opposite side of beg ch, dc in each of next 3 chs, hdc in each of next 4 chs, sc in each of next 3 chs. Fasten off.

Row 2: With RS facing, join white in first sc of row 1, ch 1, sc in same sc as joining, sc in each of next

10 sts, 2 hdc in next st, 3 hdc in next st, 2 hdc in next st, sc in each of next 11 sts. Fasten off.

OUTER EAR
Make 2.
Row 1 (RS): With size G hook and white, ch 12, sc in 2nd ch from hook, sc in each of next 2 chs, hdc in each of next 4 chs, dc in each of next 3 chs, 5 dc in last ch, working in unused lps on opposite side of beg ch, dc in each of next 3 chs, hdc in each of next 4 chs, sc in each of next 3 chs, turn.

Row 2: Ch 1, sc in each of first 11 sts, 2 hdc in next st, 3 hdc in next st, 2 hdc in next st, sc in each of next 11 sts, turn.

Row 3: Ch 1, with Inner Ear facing and outer Ear on bottom, working through both thicknesses at same time, sl st in each st around. Fasten off.

Sew Ears to top of Head.

FACE

Using satin stitch, with tapestry needle and black, embroider sts over rnds 8 and 9 of Head for eyes, as shown in photo.

Sew 2 white pompoms side by side below each eye over rnd 11.

For whiskers, cut 4 lengths of white sewing thread each 6 inches long. Pull threads through the st just above and between cheeks; tie tightly. Trim ends.

Sew pink pompom above and between cheeks over whiskers for nose.

FINISHING

Sew rem white pompom to back of Body for tail.

Tie satin ribbon around neckline in a bow. ■

Jointed
Puppy
& Bunny

DESIGNS BY CYNTHIA HARRIS

PUPPY
SKILL LEVEL

EASY

FINISHED SIZE
Approximately 16 inches tall in sitting position and 25 inches tall in standing position

MATERIALS

- Red Heart Super Saver medium (worsted) weight yarn (7 oz/364 yds/198g per skein):
  3 skeins #311 white
  2 oz/100 yds/56g #312 black
  ¼ oz/25 yds/14g #319 cherry red
- Red Heart Classic medium (worsted) weight yarn (3½ oz/190 yds/99g per skein):
  2 skeins #339 mid brown
- Sizes G/6/4mm and K/10½/6.5mm crochet hooks or sizes needed to obtain gauge
- Tapestry needle
- 8 white 1¼-inch buttons
- 1 yd 1-inch-wide red ribbon
- Polyester fiberfill

GAUGE
Size G hook: 4 sc = 1 inch; 4 sc rows = 1 inch

Size K hook and 2 strands held tog: 3 sts = 1¼ inches; 3 sc rnds = 1¼ inches.

PATTERN NOTES
Puppy is worked in continuous rounds. Do not join unless specified; mark beginning of rounds.

Weave in ends as work progresses.

Join with slip stitch as indicated unless otherwise stated.

Use a separate ball of yarn for each section of color and fasten off each color when no longer needed.

INSTRUCTIONS
BODY
Rnd 1 (RS): With size K hook and 2 strands of white, ch 3, **join** (see Pattern Notes) in first ch to form a ring, ch 1, 2 sc in each ch around. (6 sc)

Rnd 2: 2 sc in each sc around. (12 sc)

Rnd 3: [Sc in next sc, 2 sc in next sc] 9 times. (18 sc)

Rnd 4: [Sc in each of next 2 sc, 2 sc in next st] 6 times. (24 sc)

Rnd 5: [Sc in each of next 3 sc, 2 sc in next sc] 6 times. *(30 sc)*

Rnd 6: [Sc in each of next 4 sc, 2 sc in next st] 6 times. *(36 sc)*

Rnd 7: [Sc in each of next 5 sc, 2 sc in next sc] 6 times. *(42 sc)*

Rnd 8: [Sc in each of next 6 sc, 2 sc in next sc] 6 times. *(48 sc)*

Rnd 9: Sc in each of next 8 sc, **change color** *(see Stitch Guide)* to 2 strands of brown in last sc, sc in each of next 4 sc, change to white in last sc, sc in each of next 5 sc, change to brown in last sc, sc in each of next 3 sc, change to white in last sc, sc in each of next 14 sc, change to brown in last sc, sc in each of next 3 sc, change to white in last sc, sc in each of next 11 sc.

Rnd 10: Sc in each of next 7 sc, change to brown in last sc, sc in each of next 7 sc, change to white in last sc, sc in each of next 4 sc, change to brown in last sc, sc in each of next 4 sc, change to white in last sc, sc in each of next 10 sc, change to brown in last sc, sc in each of next 8 sc, change to white in last sc, sc in each of next 8 sc.

Rnd 11: Sc in each of next 6 sc, change to brown in last sc, sc in each of next 11 sc, change to white in last sc, sc in next sc, change to brown in last sc, sc in each of next 5 sc, change to white in last sc, sc in each of next 9 sc, change to brown in last sc, sc in each of next 9 sc, change to white in last sc, sc in each of next 7 sc.

Rnd 12: Sc in each of next 7 sc, change to brown in last sc, sc in each of next 16 sc, change to white in last sc, sc in each of next 11 sc, change to brown in last sc, sc in each of next 8 sc, change to white in last sc, sc in each of next 6 sc.

Rnd 13: Sc in each of next 8 sc, change to brown in last sc, sc in each of next 15 sc, change to white in last sc, sc in each of next 11 sc, change to brown in last sc, sc in each of next 11 sc, change to white in last sc, sc in each of next 3 sc.

Rnd 14: Sc in each of next 11 sc, change to brown in last sc, sc in each of next 15 sc, change to white in last sc, sc in each of next 7 sc, change to brown in last sc, sc in each of next 12 sc, change to white in last sc, sc in each of next 3 sc.

Rnd 15: Sc in each of next 10 sc, change to brown in last sc, sc in each of next 16 sc, change to white in last sc, sc in each of next 8 sc, change to brown in last sc, sc in each of next 12 sc, change to white in last sc, sc in each of next 2 sc.

Rnd 16: Sc in each of next 9 sc, change to brown in last sc, sc in each of next 17 sc, change to white in last sc, sc in each of next 7 sc, change to brown in last sc, sc in each of next 14 sc, change to white in last sc, sc in next sc.

Rnd 17: Sc in each of next 7 sc, change to brown in last sc, sc in each of next 20 sc, change to white in last sc, sc in each of next 6 sc, change to brown in last sc, sc in each of next 14 sc, change to white in last sc, sc in next sc.

Rnd 18: Sc in each of next 8 sc, change to brown in last sc, sc in each of next 19 sc, change to white in last sc, sc in each of next 7 sc, change to brown in last sc, sc in each of next 13 sc, change to white in last sc, sc in next sc.

Rnd 19: Sc in each of next 8 sc, change to brown in last sc, sc in each of next 10 sc, change to white in last sc, sc in each of next 3 sc, change to brown in last sc, sc in each of next 5 sc, change to white in last sc, sc in each of next 8 sc, change to brown in last sc, sc in each of next 11 sc, change to white in last sc, sc in each of next 3 sc.

Rnd 20: Sc in each of next 12 sc, change to brown in last sc, sc in each of next 5 sc, change to white in last sc, sc in each of next 5 sc, change to brown in last sc, sc in each of next 4 sc, change to white in last sc, sc in each of next 11 sc, change to brown in last sc, sc in each of next 8 sc, change to white in last sc, sc in each of next 3 sc.

Rnd 21: Sc in each of next 13 sc, change to brown in last sc, sc in each of next 4 sc, change to white in last sc, sc in each of next 23 sc, change to brown in last sc, sc in each of next 4 sc, change to white in last sc, sc in each of next 4 sc.

Rnd 22: Sc in each of next 16 sc, change to brown in last sc, sc in next sc, change to white, sc in each of next 25 sc, change to brown in last sc, sc in each of next 2 sc, change to white in last sc, sc in each of next 4 sc.

Rnd 23: [Sc in each of next 6 sc, **sc dec** (*see Stitch Guide*) in next 2 sc] 6 times. *(42 sc)*

Rnd 24: [Sc in each of next 5 sc, sc dec in next 2 sc] 6 times. *(36 sc)*

Rnd 25: [Sc in each of next 4 sc, sc dec in next 2 sc] 6 times. *(30 sc)*

Rnd 26: [Sc in each of next 3 sc, sc dec in next 2 sc] 6 times. *(24 sc)*

Rnd 27: [Sc in each of next 2 sc, sc dec in next 2 sc] 6 times. Leaving a 12-inch end for sewing, fasten off. *(18 sc)*

FIRST LEG
Rnd 1 (RS): With 2 strands of white, ch 3, join in first ch to form a ring, ch 1, 2 sc in each ch around. *(6 sc)*

Rnd 2: 2 sc in each sc around. *(12 sc)*

Rnd 3: 2 sc in next sc, sc in next sc, change to 2 strands of brown, sc in same sc as last sc made, 2 sc in each of next 2 sc, change to white in last sc, 2 sc in each of next 8 sc. *(24 sc)*

Rnd 4: Sc in each of next 2 sc, 2 sc in next sc, change to brown in last sc, sc in each of next 2 sc, 2 sc in next sc, sc in each of next 2 sc, 2 sc in next sc, change to white in last sc, sc in each of next 2 sc, 2 sc in next sc, sc in each of next 2 sc, 2 sc in next sc, change to brown in last sc, sc in each of next 2 sc, 2 sc in next sc, change to white in last sc, [sc in each of next 2 sc, 2 sc in next sc] twice. *(32 sc)*

Rnd 5: Sc in each of next 3 sc, 2 sc in next sc, sc in each of next 2 sc, change to brown in last sc, sc in next sc, 2 sc in next sc, sc in each of next 3 sc, sc in next sc, change to white, sc in same sc as last sc made, sc in each of next 3 sc, 2 sc in next sc, sc in each of next 3 sc, 2 sc in sc, change to brown in last sc, sc in each of next 3 sc, 2 sc in next sc, change to white in last sc, [sc in each of next 3 sc, 2 sc in next sc] twice. *(40 sc)*

Rnd 6: Sc in each of next 9 sc, change to brown in last sc, sc in each of next 4 sc, change to white in last sc, sc in each of next 12 sc, change to brown in last sc, sc in each of next 8 sc, change to white in last sc, sc in each of next 7 sc.

Rnd 7: Sc in each of next 25 sc, change to brown in last sc, sc in each of next 8 sc, change to white in last sc, sc in each of next 7 sc.

Rnd 8: [Sc dec in next 2 sc] 10 times, sc in each of next 8 sc, change to brown in last sc, sc in each of next 4 sc, change to white in last sc, sc in each of next 8 sc. *(30 sc)*

Rnd 9: Sc in each sc around.

Rnd 10: Sc in each of next 4 sc, change to brown in last sc, sc in each of next 2 sc, change to white in last sc, sc in each of next 24 sc.

Rnd 11: Sc in each of next 3 sc, change to brown in last sc, sc in each of next 5 sc, change to white in last sc, sc in each of next 22 sc.

Rnd 12: Sc in each of next 3 sc, change to brown in last sc, sc in each of next 8 sc, change to white in last sc, sc in each of next 19 sc.

Rnd 13: Sc in each of next 3 sc, change to brown in last sc, sc in each of next 8 sc, change to white in last sc, sc in each of next 19 sc.

Rnd 14: Sc in each of next 6 sc, change to brown in last sc, sc in each of next 5 sc, change to white in last sc, sc in each of next 19 sc.

Rnd 15: Sc in each of next 8 sc, change to brown in last sc, sc in each of next 2 sc, change to white in last sc, sc in each of next 9 sc in last sc, change to brown, sc in each of next 3 sc, change to white in last sc, sc in each of next 8 sc.

Rnd 16: Sc in each of next 19 sc, change to brown in last sc, sc in each of next 6 sc, change to white in last sc, sc in each of next 5 sc.

Rnd 17: Sc in each of next 19 sc, change to brown in last sc, sc in each of next 7 sc, change to white in last sc, sc in each of next 4 sc.

Rnd 18: Sc in next sc, change to brown, sc in each of next 8 sc, change to white in last sc, sc in each of next 4 sc.

Rnd 19: Sc in each of next 4 sc, change to brown in last sc, sc in each of next 2 sc, change to white in last sc, sc in each of next 13 sc, change to brown in last sc, sc in each of next 6 sc, change to white in last sc, sc in each of next 5 sc.

Rnd 20: Sc in each of next 4 sc, change to brown in last sc, sc in each of next 4 sc, change to white in last sc, sc in each of next 12 sc, change to brown in last sc, sc in each of next 7 sc, change to white in last sc, sc in each of next 3 sc.

Rnd 21: Sc in each of next 4 sc, change to brown in last sc, sc in each of next 6 sc, change to white in last sc, sc in each of next 13 sc, change to brown in last sc, sc in each of next 4 sc, change to white in last sc, sc in each of next 3 sc.

Rnd 22: Sc in each of next 4 sc, change to brown in last sc, sc in each of next 7 sc, change to white in last sc, sc in each of next 15 sc, change to brown in last sc, sc in each of next 2 sc, change to white in last sc, sc in each of next 2 sc.

Rnd 23: Sc in each of next 3 sc, change to brown in last sc, sc in each of next 6 sc, change to white in last sc, sc in each of next 21 sc.

Rnd 24: Sc in each of next 3 sc, change to brown in last sc, sc in each of next 7 sc, change to white in last sc, sc in each of next 20 sc.

Rnd 25: Sc in each of next 6 sc, change to brown in last sc, sc in each of next 4 sc, change to white in last sc, sc in each of next 20 sc.

Rnd 26: Sc in each of next 8 sc, change to brown in last sc, sc in each of next 2 sc, change to white in last sc, sc in each of next 9 sc, change to brown in last sc, sc in each of next 2 sc, change to white, sc in each of next 9 sc.

Rnd 27: Sc in each of next 18 sc, change to brown in last sc, sc in each of next 5 sc, change to white in last sc, sc in each of next 7 sc.

Rnd 28: Sc in each of next 18 sc, change to brown in last sc, sc in each of next 5 sc, change to white in last sc, sc in each of next 7 sc.

Rnd 29: [Sc in each of next 3 sc, sc dec in next 2 sc] 3 times, sc in each of next 3 sc, change to brown in last sc, sc dec in next 2 sc, sc in each of next 3 sc, change to white in last sc, sc dec in next 2 sc, sc in each of next 3 sc, sc dec in next 2 sc. (*24 sc*)

Rnd 30: [Sc in each of next 2 sc, sc dec in next 2 sc] 6 times. (*18 sc*)

Rnd 31: [Sc in next sc, sc dec in next 2 sc] 6 times. (*12 sc*)

Rnd 32: [Sc dec in next 2 sc] 6 times. Leaving a 12-inch end for sewing, fasten off. (*6 sc*)

Stuff. Sew opening closed.

2ND LEG
Rnd 1 (RS): With size K hook and 2 strands of white, ch 3, join in first ch to form a ring, ch 1, 2 sc in each ch around. (*6 sc*)

Rnd 2: 2 sc in each sc around. (*12 sc*)

Rnd 3: 2 sc in each sc around. (*24 sc*)

Rnd 4: [Sc in each of next 2 sc, 2 sc in next sc] 8 times. (*32 sc*)

Rnd 5: [Sc in each of next 3 sc, 2 sc in next sc] twice, sc in next sc, change to brown, sc in each of next 2 sc, 2 sc in next sc, change to white in last sc, [sc in each of next 3 sc, 2 sc in next sc] twice, sc in each of next 2 sc, change to brown in last sc, sc in next sc, 2 sc in next sc, change to white in last sc, [sc in each of next 3 sc, 2 sc in next sc] twice. (*40 sc*)

Rnd 6: Sc in each of next 11 sc, change to brown in last sc, sc in each of next 6 sc, change to white in last sc, sc in each of next 9 sc, change to brown in last sc, sc in each of next 6 sc, change to white in last sc, sc in each of next 8 sc.

Rnd 7: Sc in each of next 11 sc, change to brown in last sc, sc in each of next 5 sc, change to white in last sc, sc in each of next 8 sc, change to brown in last sc, sc in each of next 9 sc, change to white in last sc, sc in each of next 7 sc.

Rnd 8: [Sc dec in next 2 sc] 6 times, sc dec in next 2 sc, change to brown, sc dec in next 2 sc, sc dec in next 2 sc, change to white, sc dec in next 2 sc, sc in each of next 6 sc, change to brown in last sc, sc in each of next 8 sc, change to white in last sc, sc in each of next 6 sc. *(30 sc)*

Rnd 9: Sc in each of next 19 sc, change to brown in last sc, sc in each of next 5 sc, change to white in last sc, sc in each of next 6 sc.

Rnd 10: Sc in each of next 22 sc, change to brown in last sc, sc in each of next 2 sc, change to white in last sc, sc in each of next 6 sc.

Rnd 11: Sc in each of next 28 sc, change to brown in last sc, sc in each of next 2 sc.

Rnd 12: Sc in each of next 3 sc, change to white in last sc, sc in each of next 25 sc, change to brown in last sc, sc in each of next 2 sc.

Rnd 13: Sc in each of next 4 sc, change to white in last sc, sc in each of next 24 sc, change to brown in last sc, sc in each of next 2 sc.

Rnd 14: Sc in each of next 7 sc, change to white in last sc, sc in each of next 21 sc, change to brown in last sc, sc in each of next 2 sc.

Rnd 15: Sc in each of next 7 sc, change to white in last sc, sc in each of next 20 sc, change to brown in last sc, sc in each of next 3 sc.

Rnd 16: Sc in each of next 10 sc, change to white in last sc, sc in each of next 18 sc, change to brown in last sc, sc in each of next 2 sc.

Rnd 17: Sc in each of next 4 sc, change to white in last sc, sc in each of next 2 sc, change to brown in last sc, sc in each of next 4 sc, change to white in last sc, sc in each of next 20 sc.

Rnd 18: Sc in next sc, change to brown, sc in each of next 3 sc, change to white in last sc, sc in each of next 3 sc, change to brown in last sc, sc in each of next 3 sc, change to white in last sc, sc in each of next 20 sc.

Rnd 19: Sc in each of next 7 sc, change to brown in last sc, sc in each of next 3 sc, change to white, sc in each of next 8 sc, change to brown in last sc, sc in each of next 2 sc, change to white in last sc, sc in each of next 10 sc.

Rnd 20: Sc in each of next 18 sc, change to brown in last sc, sc in each of next 3 sc, change to white in last sc, sc in each of next 9 sc.

Rnd 21: Sc in each of next 18 sc, change to brown in last sc, sc in each of next 5 sc, change to white in last sc, sc in each of next 7 sc.

Rnd 22: Sc in each of next 14 sc, change to brown in last sc, sc in each of next 3 sc, change to white in last sc, sc in each of next 2 sc, change to brown in last sc, sc in each of next 6 sc, change to white in last sc, sc in each of next 5 sc.

Rnd 23: Sc in each of next 14 sc, change to brown in last sc, sc in each of next 11 sc, change to white in last sc, sc in each of next 5 sc.

Rnd 24: Sc in each of next 15 sc, change to brown in last sc, sc in each of next 10 sc, change to white in last sc, sc in each of next 5 sc.

Rnd 25: Sc in each of next 5 sc, change to brown in last sc, sc in each of next 3 sc, change to white in last sc, sc in each of next 9 sc, change to brown in last sc, sc in each of next 6 sc, change to white in last sc, sc in each of next 7 sc.

Rnd 26: Sc in each of next 5 sc, change to brown in last sc, sc in each of next 5 sc, change to white in last sc, sc in each of next 10 sc, change to brown in last sc, sc in each of next 3 sc, change to white in last sc, sc in each of next 7 sc.

Rnd 27: Sc in each of next 5 sc, change to brown in last sc, sc in each of next 7 sc, change to white in last sc, sc in each of next 18 sc.

Rnd 28: Sc in each of next 7 sc, change to brown in last sc, sc in each of next 5 sc, change to white in last sc, sc in each of next 18 sc.

Rnd 29: Sc in each of next 3 sc, sc dec in next 2 sc, sc in each of next 3 sc, change to brown, sc dec in next 2 sc, sc in next sc, change to white, sc in each of next 2 sc, sc dec in next 2 sc, [sc in each of next 3 sc, sc dec in next 2 sc] 3 times. *(24 sc)*

Rnd 30: [Sc in each of next 2 sts, sc dec in next 2 sc] 6 times. *(18 sc)*

Rnd 31: [Sc in next sc, sc dec in next 2 sc] 6 times. *(12 sc)*

Rnd 32: [Sc dec in next 2 sc] 6 times. Leaving a 12-inch end for sewing, fasten off. *(6 sc)*

Stuff. Sew opening closed.

ARM
Make 2.
Rnd 1: With size K hook and 2 strands of white, ch 3, join in first ch to form a ring, ch 1, 2 sc in each ch around. *(6 sc)*

Rnd 2: 2 sc in each sc around. *(12 sc)*

Rnd 3: [Sc in next sc, 2 sc in next sc] 6 times. *(18 sc)*

Rnd 4: [Sc in each of next 2 sc, 2 sc in next sc] 6 times. *(24 sc)*

Rnd 5: Sc in each of next 3 sc, change to brown, sc in each of next 3 sc, change to white, sc in each of next 18 sc.

Rnd 6: Sc in each of next 2 sc, change to brown in last sc, sc in each of next 7 sc, change to white, sc in each of next 8 sc, change to brown, sc in each of next 2 sc, change to white, sc in each of next 5 sc.

Rnd 7: Sc in each of next 2 sc, change to brown, sc in each of next 7 sc, change to white in last sc, sc in each of next 7 sc, change to brown in last sc, sc in each of next 5 sc, change to white in last sc, sc in each of next 3 sc.

Rnd 8: Sc in each of next 4 sc, change to brown in last sc, sc in each of next 5 sc, change to white in last sc, sc in each of next 7 sc, change to brown in last sc, sc in each of next 5 sc, change to white in last sc, sc in each of next 3 sc.

Rnd 9: Sc in each of next 5 sc, change to brown, sc in each of next 4 sc, change to white in last sc, sc in each of next 7 sc, change to brown in last sc, sc in each of next 7 sc, change to white in last sc, sc in next sc.

Rnd 10: Sc in each of next 7 sc, change to brown in last sc, sc in each of next 2 sc, change to white in last sc, sc in each of next 7 sc, change to brown in last sc, sc in each of next 7 sc, change to white in last sc, sc in next sc.

Rnd 11: Sc in each of next 17 sc, change to brown in last sc, sc in each of next 5 sc, change to white in last sc, sc in each of next 2 sc.

Rnd 12: Sc in each of next 21 sc, change to brown in last sc, sc in next sc, change to white in last sc, sc in each of next 2 sc.

Rnds 13 & 14: Sc in each sc around.

Rnd 15: Sc in each of next 4 sc, change to brown in last sc, sc in each of next 2 sc, change to white in last sc, sc in each of next 18 sc.

Rnd 16: Sc in each of next 4 sc, change to brown in last sc, sc in each of next 5 sc, change to white in last sc, sc in each of next 15 sc.

Rnd 17: Sc in each of next 4 sc, change to brown in last sc, sc in each of next 8 sc, change to white in last sc, sc in each of next 12 sc.

Rnd 18: Sc in each of next 6 sc, change to brown in last sc, sc in each of next 8 sc, change to white in last sc, sc in each of next 6 sc, change to brown in last sc, sc in each of next 2 sc, change to white in last sc, sc in each of next 2 sc.

Rnd 19: Sc in each of next 6 sc, change to brown in last sc, sc in each of next 8 sc, change to white in last sc, sc in each of next 5 sc, change to brown in last sc, sc in each of next 4 sc, change to white in last sc, sc in next sc.

Rnd 20: Sc in each of next 7 sc, change to brown in last sc, sc in each of next 6 sc, change to white in last sc, sc in each of next 6 sc, change to brown in last sc, sc in each of next 4 sc, change to white in last sc, sc in next sc.

Rnd 21: Sc in each of next 6 sc, change to brown in last sc, sc in each of next 7 sc, change to white in last sc, sc in each of next 8 sc, change to brown in last sc, sc in each of next 2 sc, change to white in last sc, sc in next sc.

Rnd 22: Sc in each of next 7 sc, change to brown in last sc, sc in each of next 5 sc, change to white in last sc, sc in each of next 12 sc.

Rnd 23: Sc in each of next 10 sc, change to brown in last sc, sc in each of next 2 sc, change to white in last sc, sc in each of next 12 sc.

Rnd 24: Sc in each sc around.

Rnd 25: [Sc in each of next 2 sc, dc dec in next 2 sc] 6 times. *(18 sc)*

Rnd 26: [Sc in next sc, sc dec in next 2 sc] 6 times. *(12 sc)*

Rnd 27: [Sc dec in next 2 sc] 6 times. Leaving a 12-inch end for sewing, fasten off. *(6 sc)*

Stuff firmly. Sew opening closed.

HEAD
Rnd 1 (RS): With size K hook and 2 strands of white, ch 3, join in first ch to form a ring, ch 1, 2 sc in each ch around. *(6 sc)*

Rnd 2: 2 sc in each sc around. *(12 sc)*

Rnd 3: 2 sc in next sc, change to brown in last sc, 2 sc in next sc, sc in next sc, change to white, sc in same sc as last sc made, 2 sc in each of next 3 sc, sc in next sc, change to brown, sc in same sc as last sc made, sc in next sc, change to white, sc in same sc as last sc made, 2 sc in each of next 4 sc. *(24 sc)*

Rnd 4: Sc in each of next 3 sc, change to brown in last sc, 2 sc in next sc, sc in each of next 2 sc, change to white in last sc, sc in next sc, 2 sc in next sc, sc in each of next 4 sc, change to brown in last sc, sc in same sc as last sc made, sc in each of next 3 sc, 2 sc in next sc, change to white in last sc, [sc in each of next 3 sc, 2 sc in next sc] twice. *(30 sc)*

Rnd 5: Sc in each of next 3 sc, change to brown in last sc, sc in next sc, 2 sc in next sc, sc in each of next 4 sc, change to white in last sc, 2 sc in next sc, sc in each of next 5 sc, change to brown in last sc, sc in same sc as last sc made, sc in each of next 4 sc, 2 sc in next sc, sc in next sc, change to white, sc in each of next 3 sc, 2 sc in next sc, sc in each of next 4 sc, 2 sc in next sc. *(36 sc)*

Rnd 6: Sc in each of next 5 sc, change to brown in last sc, 2 sc in next sc, sc in each of next 4 sc, change to white in last sc, sc in next sc, 2 sc in next sc, sc in each of next 5 sc, 2 sc in next sc, change to brown in last sc, sc in each of next 5 sc, 2 sc in next sc, sc in each of next 4 sc, change to white in last sc, sc in next sc, 2 sc in next sc, sc in each of next 5 sc, 2 sc in next sc. *(42 sc)*

Rnd 7: Sc in each of next 6 sc, change to brown in last sc, sc in each of next 5 sc, change to white in last sc, sc in each of next 12 sc, change to brown in last sc, sc in each of next 9 sc, change to white in last sc, sc in each of next 10 sc.

Rnd 8: Sc in each of next 7 sc, change to brown in last sc, sc in each of next 3 sc, change to white in last sc, sc in each of next 14 sc, change to brown in last sc, sc in each of next 8 sc, change to white in last sc, sc in each of next 10 sc.

Rnd 9: Sc in each of next 23 sc, change to brown in last sc, sc in each of next 9 sc, change to white in last sc, sc in each of next 10 sc.

Rnd 10: [Sc in each of next 6 sc, 2 sc in next sc] 3 times, sc in each of next 2 sc, change to brown in last sc, sc in each of next 4 sc, 2 sc in next sc, sc in each of next 3 sc, change to white in last sc, sc in each of next 3 sc, 2 sc in next sc, sc in each of next 6 sc, 2 sc in next sc. *(48 sc)*

Rnd 11: Sc in each of next 26 sc, change to brown in last sc, sc in each of next 4 sc, change to white in last sc, sc in each of next 2 sc, change to brown in last sc, sc in each of next 3 sc, change to white in last sc, sc in each of next 8 sc, change to brown in last sc, sc in each of next 3 sc, change to white in last sc, sc in each of next 2 sc.

Rnd 12: Sc in each of next 33 sc, change to brown in last sc, sc in each of next 2 sc, change to white in last sc, sc in each of next 6 sc, change to brown in last sc, sc in each of next 6 sc, change to white in last sc, sc in next sc.

Rnd 13: Sc in each of next 19 sc, change to brown in last sc, sc in each of next 2 sc, change to white in last sc, sc in each of next 20 sc, change to brown in last sc, sc in each of next 7 sc.

Rnd 14: Sc in each of next 2 sc, change to white in last sc, sc in each of next 5 sc, 2 sc in next sc, sc in each of next 7 sc, change to brown in last sc, 2 sc in next sc, change to white in last sc, sc in each of next 3 sc, change to brown in last sc, sc in each of next 4 sc, change to white, [2 sc in next sc, sc in each of next 7 sc] twice, 2 sc in next sc, sc in each of next 3 sc, change to brown in last sc, sc in each of next 4 sc, 2 sc in next sc. *(54 sc)*

Rnd 15: Sc in each of next 3 sc, change to white in last sc, sc in each of next 13 sc, change to brown in last sc, sc in each of next 10 sc, change to white in last sc, sc in each of next 25 sc, change to brown in last sc, sc in each of next 3 sc.

Rnd 16: Sc in each of next 2 sc, change to white in last sc, sc in each of next 16 sc, change to brown in last sc, sc in each of next 8 sc, change to white in last sc, sc in each of next 26 sc, change to brown in last sc, sc in each of next 2 sc.

Rnd 17: Sc in each of next 2 sc, change to white in last sc, sc in each of next 17 sc, change to brown in last sc, sc in each of next 6 sc, change to white in last sc, sc in each of next 29 sc.

Rnd 18: Sc in each of next 20 sc, change to brown in last sc, sc in each of next 4 sc, change to white in last sc, sc in each of next 30 sc.

Rnd 19: Sc in each of next 44 sc, change to brown in last sc, sc in each of next 3 sc, change to white in last sc, sc in each of next 7 sc.

Rnd 20: Sc in each of next 43 sc, change to brown in last sc, sc in each of next 6 sc, change to white in last sc, sc in each of next 5 sc.

Rnd 21: [Sc in each of next 7 sc, sc dec in next 2 sc] 4 times, sc in each of next 7 sc, change to brown in last sc, 2 sc in next sc, sc in each of next 4 sc, change to white in last sc, sc in each of next 3 sc, 2 sc in next sc. *(48 sc)*

Rnd 22: [Sc in each of next 6 sc, sc dec in next 2 sc] 5 times, sc in next sc, change to brown, sc in each of next 3 sc, change to white in last sc, sc in each of next 2 sc, 2 sc in next sc. *(42 sc)*

Rnd 23: [Sc in each of next 5 sc, sc dec in next 2 sc] 6 times. *(36 sc)*

Rnd 24: [Sc in each of next 4 sc, sc dec in next 2 sc] 6 times. *(30 sc)*

Rnd 25: [Sc in each of next 3 sc, sc dec in next 2 sc] 6 times. Leaving a 12-inch end for sewing, fasten off. *(24 sc)*

Stuff firmly.

ASSEMBLY

Step 1: Flatten top of 1 Leg so indentations are on inner and outer sides and toe shaping is pointing forward.

Step 2: With tapestry needle and double strand of white 24 inches long, pull yarn through holes on first button with long ends of yarn pulled even on WS.

Step 3: Making certain both ends of yarn go through same sp (this allows Leg to be fully jointed), insert ends on first button through same sp between 5th and 6th rnds from top of Leg working from outer side to inner side, then through same sp between rnds 11 and 12 on Body. Pull ends of yarn through 2nd button on inside of Body, pull tight so Leg will indent *(see photo)*. Secure ends on inside of Body.

Step 4: Rep with other Leg on opposite side of Body, making certain toes of both Legs are pointing in same direction.

Step 5: Flatten top of 1 Arm so indentations are on inner and outer sides.

Step 6: Making certain both ends of yarn go through the same sp, insert ends on first button through same sp between 4th and 5th rnds from top of Arm working from outer side to inner side; then through same sp between rnds 25 and 26 on Body, making certain arm is attached directly above Leg. Pull ends of yarn through 2nd button on inside of Body, pull tight so Arm will indent *(see photo)*. Secure ends on inside of Body.

Step 7: Rep with other Arm on opposite side of Body,

Step 8: Stuff Body firmly. With long end, sew Body closed.

Step 9: Sew last rnd on Head to top of Body.

MUZZLE

Rnd 1 (RS): With size K hook and 2 strands of white, ch 3, join in first ch to form a ring, ch 1, 2 sc in each ch around. (6 sc)

Rnd 2: 2 sc in each st around. *(12 sc)*

Rnd 3: Sc in each of next 2 sc, change to brown, sc in same sc as last sc made, sc in each of next 2 sc, change to white in last sc, sc in same sc as last sc made, sc in next sc, 2 sc in next sc, sc in each of next 2 sc, change to brown in last sc, sc in same sc as last sc made, sc in next sc, change to white, 2 sc in next sc, sc in next sc, 2 sc in next sc. *(18 sc)*

Rnd 4: Sc in each of next 3 sc, change to brown in last sc, sc in same sc as last sc made, sc in each of next 3 sc, change to white in last sc, sc in same sc as last sc made, sc in each of next 2 sc, 2 sc in next sc, sc in each of next 2 sc, change to brown in last sc, 2 sc in next sc, sc in each of next 2 sc, change to white in last sc, 2 sc in next sc, sc in each of next 2 sc, 2 sc in next sc. *(24 sc)*

Rnd 5: Sc in each of next 4 sc, change to brown in last sc, sc in same sc as last sc made, sc in each of next 3 sc, 2 sc in next sc, change to white in last sc, sc in each of next 3 sc, 2 sc in next sc, sc in each of next 3 sc, 2 sc in next sc, change to brown in last sc, sc in each of next 2 sc, change to white in last sc, sc in next sc, 2 sc in next sc, sc in each of next 3 sc, 2 sc in next sc. *(30 sc)*

Rnd 6: Sc in each of next 5 sc, change to brown in last sc, sc in same sc as last sc made, sc in each of next 4 sc, 2 sc in next sc, change to white in last sc, [sc in each of next 4 sc, 2 sc in next sc] 4 times. *(36 sc)*

Rnd 7: Sc in each of next 9 sc, change to brown in last sc, sc in each of next 2 sc, change to white in last sc, sc in each of next 25 sc.

Rnd 8: Sc in each sc around.

Rnd 9: [Sc in each of next 4 sc, sc dec in next 2 sc] 6 times. *(30 sc)*

Rnd 10: Sc in each sc around. Leaving a 12-inch end for sewing, fasten off.

Stuff firmly. Sew Muzzle to Head over rnds 15–23.

NOSE

Rnd 1 (RS): With size K hook and 2 strands of black, ch 3, join in first ch to form a ring, ch 1, 2 sc in each ch around. *(6 sc)*

Rnd 2: 2 sc in each sc around. *(12 sc)*

Rnd 3: Sc in each sc around.

Rnd 4: [Sc dec in next 2 sc] 6 times. Leaving a 12-inch end for sewing, fasten off.

Stuff firmly. Sew Nose to rnd 6 of Muzzle.

Using **straight stitch** *(see Fig. 1)*, with tapestry needle and 2 strands of black and beg under Nose, work a 1-inch vertical st.

Fig. 1
Straight Stitch

TONGUE

With size G hook and 1 strand of red, ch 5, sc in 2nd ch from hook, sc in next ch, hdc in next ch, 6 dc in last ch, working in unused lps on opposite side of starting ch, hdc in next ch, sc in each of next 2 chs. Leaving a 12-inch end for sewing, fasten off.

Sew end with sc at bottom of vertical st under Nose *(see photo)*.

EAR
Make 2.
Rnd 1 (RS): With size K hook and 2 strands of black, ch 3, join in first ch to form a ring, ch 1, 2 sc in each ch around. *(6 sc)*

Rnd 2: 2 sc in each sc around. *(12 sc)*

Rnd 3: [Sc in next sc, 2 sc in next sc] 6 times. *(18 sc)*

Rnds 4 & 5: Sc in each sc around.

Rnd 6: [Sc in each of next 7 sc, sc dec in next 2 sc] twice. *(16 sc)*

Rnds 7–9: Sc in each sc around.

Rnd 10: [Sc in each of next 6 sc, sc dec in next 2 sc] twice. *(14 sc)*

Rnds 11–13: Sc in each sc around.

Rnd 14: [Sc in each of next 5 sc, sc dec in next 2 sc] twice. *(12 sc)*

Rnds 15–17: Sc in each sc around.

Rnd 18: [Sc in each of next 4 sc, sc dec in next 2 sc] twice. *(10 sc)*

Rnds 19–21: Sc in each sc around.

Flatten rnd 21. Working through both thicknesses at same time, sc in each sc across. Leaving a 12-inch end for sewing, fasten off.

Sew Ear between rnds 5–6 so Ear flops down side of Head. Rep with other Ear on opposite side.

EYE
Make 2.
With size G hook and 1 strand of black, ch 2, 7 hdc in 2nd ch from hook, join in 2nd ch of beg ch-2. Leaving a 12-inch end for sewing, fasten off.

Working in **back lps** *(see Stitch Guide)* only, sew to Head above Muzzle 1 inch apart.

TAIL
Rnd 1 (RS): With size K hook and 2 strands of black, ch 2, 4 sc in 2nd ch from hook. *(4 sc)*

Rnd 2: 2 sc in next sc, sc in each of next 3 sc. *(5 sc)*

Rnd 3: Sc in each sc around.

Rnd 4: 2 sc in next sc, sc in each of next 4 sc. *(6 sc)*

Rnds 5–10: Rep rnd 3.

Rnd 11: 2 sc in next sc, sc in each of next 5 sc. *(7 sc)*

Rnds 12–14: Rep rnd 3.

Rnd 15: 2 sc in next sc, sc in each of next 6 sc. *(8 sc)*

Rnds 16–18: Rep rnd 3.

Rnd 19: [Sc in each of next 3 sc, 2 sc in next sc] twice. *(10 sc)*

Rnd 20: [Sc in each of next 4 sc, 2 sc in next sc] twice. *(12 sc)*

Rnd 21: [Sc in each of next 5 sc, 2 sc in next sc] twice. *(14 sc)*

Rnd 22: [Sc in each of next 6 sc, 2 sc in next sc] twice. Leaving a 12-inch end for sewing, fasten off.

Stuff firmly. With Body in sitting position, sew Tail to back of Body at center bottom.

FINISHING
Using straight stitch and 1 strand of black, embroider 4 long sts over end of each Arm and each Leg.

Tie ribbon in bow around neck.

BUNNY
SKILL LEVEL

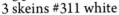

EASY

FINISHED SIZE
Approximately 16 inches tall in sitting position and 25 inches tall in standing position

MATERIALS
- Red Heart Super Saver medium (worsted) weight yarn (7 oz/364 yds/ 198g per skein):
  - 3 skeins #311 white
  - 2 oz/100 yds/56g each #373 petal pink and #312 black
- Sizes G/6/4mm and K/10½/6.5mm crochet hooks or sizes needed to obtain gauge
- Tapestry needle
- 8 white 1¼-inch buttons
- 1 yd 1¼-inch-wide pink and white gingham ribbon
- Polyester fiberfill

GAUGE
Size G hook and 1 strand: 4 sc = 1 inch; 4 sc rows = 1 inch.

Size K hook and 2 strands held tog: 3 sts = 1¼ inches; 3 sc rnds = 1¼ inches.

PATTERN NOTES
Bunny is worked in continuous rounds. Do not join unless specified; mark beginning of rounds.

Weave in ends as work progresses.

Join with slip stitch as indicated unless otherwise stated.

INSTRUCTIONS
BODY
Rnd 1 (RS): With size K hook and 2 strands of white, ch 3, **join** *(see Pattern Notes)* in first ch to form a ring, ch 1, 2 sc in each ch around. *(6 sc)*

Rnd 2: 2 sc in each sc around. *(12 sc)*

Rnd 3: [Sc in next sc, 2 sc in next sc] 6 times. *(18 sc)*

Rnd 4: [Sc in each of next 2 sc, 2 sc in next st] 6 times. *(24 sc)*

Rnd 5: [Sc in each of next 3 sc, 2 sc in next sc] 6 times. *(30 sc)*

Rnd 6: [Sc in each of next 4 sc, 2 sc in next st] 6 times. *(36 sc)*

Rnd 7: [Sc in each of next 5 sc, 2 sc in next sc] 6 times. *(42 sc)*

Rnd 8: [Sc in each of next 6 sc, 2 sc in next sc] 6 times. *(48 sc)*

Rnds 9–22: Sc in each sc around.

Rnd 23: [Sc in each of next 6 sc, **sc dec** *(see Stitch Guide)* in next 2 sc] 6 times. *(42 sc)*

Rnd 24: [Sc in each of next 5 sc, sc dec in next 2 sc] 6 times. *(36 sc)*

Rnd 25: [Sc in each of next 4 sc, sc dec in next 2 sc] 6 times. *(30 sc)*

Rnd 26: [Sc in each of next 3 sc, sc dec in next 2 sc] 6 times. *(24 sc)*

Rnd 27: [Sc in each of next 2 sc, sc dec in next 2 sc] 6 times. Leaving a 12-inch end for sewing, fasten off. *(18 sc)*

Note: Do not stuff Body until later during Assembly.

LEG
Make 2.

Rnd 1 (RS): With size K hook and 2 strands of white, ch 3, join in first ch to form a ring, ch 1, 2 sc in each ch around. *(6 sc)*

Rnd 2: 2 sc in each sc around. *(12 sc)*

Rnd 3: 2 sc in each sc around. *(24 sc)*

Rnd 4: [Sc in each of next 2 sc, 2 sc in next sc] 8 times. *(32 sc)*

Rnd 5: [Sc in each of next 3 sc, 2 sc in next sc] 8 times. *(40 sc)*

Rnds 6 & 7: Sc in each sc around.

Rnd 8: [Sc dec in next 2 sc] 10 times *(toe shaping)*, sc in each of next 20 sc. *(30 sc)*

Rnds 9–28: Sc in each sc around.

Rnd 29: [Sc in each of next 3 sc, sc dec in next 2 sc] 6 times. *(24 sc)*

Rnd 30: [Sc in each of next 2 sc, sc dec in next 2 sc] 6 times. *(18 sc)*

Rnd 31: [Sc in next sc, sc dec in next 2 sc] 6 times. *(12 sc)*

Rnd 32: [Sc dec in next 2 sc] 6 times. Leaving a 12-inch end for sewing, fasten off. *(6 sc)*

Stuff with fiberfill. Sew opening closed.

ARM
Make 2.

Rnd 1 (RS): With size K hook and 2 strands of white, ch 3, join in first ch to form a ring, ch 1, 2 sc in each ch around. *(6 sc)*

Rnd 2: 2 sc in each st around. *(12 sc)*

Rnd 3: [Sc in next sc, 2 sc in next st] 6 times. *(18 sc)*

Rnd 4: [Sc in each of next 2 sc, 2 sc in next sc] 6 times. *(24 sc)*

Rnds 5–24: Sc in each sc around.

Rnd 25: [Sc in each of next 2 sc, sc dec in next 2 sc] 6 times. *(18 sc)*

Rnd 26: [Sc in next sc, sc dec in next 2 sc] 6 times. *(12 sc)*

Rnd 27: [Sc dec in next 2 sc] 6 times. Leaving a 12-inch end for sewing, fasten off. *(6 sc)*

Stuff with fiberfill. Sew opening closed.

HEAD

Rnd 1 (RS): With size K hook and 2 strands of white, ch 3, join in first ch to form a ring, ch 1, 2 sc in each ch around. *(6 sc)*

Rnd 2: 2 sc in each sc around. *(12 sc)*

Rnd 3: 2 sc in each sc around. *(24 sc)*

Rnd 4: [Sc in each of next 3 sc, 2 sc in next sc] 6 times. *(30 sc)*

Rnd 5: [Sc in each of next 4 sc, 2 sc in next sc] 6 times. *(36 sc)*

Rnd 6: [Sc in each of next 5 sc, 2 sc in next sc] 6 times. *(42 sc)*

Rnds 7–9: Sc in each sc around.

Rnd 10: [Sc in each of next 6 sc, 2 sc in next sc] 6 times. *(48 sc)*

Rnds 11–13: Sc in each sc around.

Rnd 14: [Sc in each of next 7 sc, 2 sc in next sc] 6 times. *(54 sc)*

Rnds 15–20: Sc in each sc around.

Rnd 21: [Sc in each of next 7 sc sc dec in next 2 sc] 6 times. *(48 sc)*

Rnd 22: [Sc in each of next 6 sc, sc dec in next 2 sc] 6 times. *(42 sc)*

Rnd 23: [Sc in each of next 5 sc, sc dec in next 2 sc] 6 times. *(36 sc)*

Rnd 24: [Sc in each of next 4 sc, sc dec in next 2 sc] 6 times. *(30 sc)*

Rnd 25: [Sc in each of next 3 sc, sc dec in next 2 sc] 6 times. Leaving a 12-inch end for sewing, fasten off. *(24 sc)*

Stuff firmly.

ASSEMBLY
Step 1: Flatten top of 1 Leg so indentations are on inner and outer sides and toe shaping is pointing forward.

Step 2: With tapestry needle and double strand of white 24 inches long, pull yarn through holes on first button with long ends of yarn pulled even on WS.

Step 3: Making certain both ends of yarn go through same sp (this allows Leg to be fully jointed), insert ends on first button through same sp between 5th and 6th rnds from top of Leg, working from outer side to inner side, then through same sp between rnds 11 and 12 on Body. Pull ends of yarn through 2nd button on inside of Body, pulling tight so Leg will indent *(see photo)*. Secure ends on inside of Body.

Step 4: Rep with other Leg on opposite side of Body, making certain toes of both Legs are pointing in same direction.

Step 5: Flatten top of 1 Arm so indentations are on inner and outer sides.

Step 6: Making certain both ends of yarn go through the same sp, insert ends on first button through same sp between 4th and 5th rnds from top of Arm, working from outer side to inner side, then through same sp between rnds 25 and 26 on Body, making certain arm is attached directly above Leg. Pull ends of yarn through 2nd button on inside of Body, pulling tight so Arm will indent *(see photo)*. Secure ends on inside of Body.

Step 7: Rep with other Arm on opposite side of Body,

Step 8: Stuff Body firmly. With long end, sew Body closed.

Step 9: Sew last rnd on Head to top of Body.

CHEEK
Make 2.
Rnd 1 (RS): With size K hook and 2 strands of white, ch 3, join in first ch to form a ring, ch 1, 2 sc in each ch around. *(6 sc)*

Rnd 2: 2 sc in each sc around. *(12 sc)*

Rnd 3: [Sc in next sc, 2 sc in next sc] 6 times. *(18 sc)*

Rnd 4: [Sc in each of next 2 sc, 2 sc in next sc] 6 times. *(24 sc)*

Rnd 5: Sc in each sc around.

Rnd 6: Sc in each sc around, join in first sc. Leaving a 12-inch end for sewing, fasten off.

EAR
Make 2.
Rnd 1 (RS): With size K hook and 2 strands of white, ch 3, join in first ch to form a ring, ch 1, 2 sc in each ch around. *(6 sc)*

Rnd 2: [Sc in each of next 2 sc, 2 sc in next sc] twice. *(8 sc)*

Rnds 3 & 4: Sc in each sc around.

Rnd 5: [Sc in each of next 3 sc, 2 sc in next sc] twice. *(10 sc)*

Rnd 6: Sc in each sc around.

Rnd 7: [Sc in each of next 4 sc, 2 sc in next sc] twice. *(12 sc)*

Rnd 8: Sc in each sc around.

Rnd 9: [Sc in each of next 5 sc, 2 sc in next sc] twice. *(14 sc)*

Rnd 10: [Sc in each of next 6 sc, 2 sc in next sc] twice. *(16 sc)*

Rnd 11: [Sc in each of next 7 sc, 2 sc in next sc] twice. *(18 sc)*

Rnd 12: [Sc in each of next 8 sc, 2 sc in next sc] twice. *(20 sc)*

Rnds 13–22: Sc in each sc around.

Rnd 23: [Sc dec in next 2 sc] 5 times, join in first sc. Leaving a 12-inch end for sewing, fasten off.

TAIL
Rnd 1 (RS): With size K hook and 2 strands of white, ch 3, join in first ch to form a ring, ch 1, 2 sc in each ch around. *(6 sc)*

*Note: Rem rnds are worked in **back lps** (see Stitch Guide) only.*

Rnd 2: 2 sc in each sc around. *(12 sc)*

Rnd 3: [Sc in next sc, 2 sc in next sc] 6 times. *(18 sc)*

Rnd 4: [Sc in each of next 2 sc, 2 sc in next sc] 6 times. *(24 sc)*

Rnd 5: [Sc in each of next 2 sc, sc dec in next 2 sc] 6 times. Leaving a 12-inch end for sewing, fasten off. *(18 sc)*

TAIL PUFF
With size K hook, join 2 strands of white with sl st in first unused lp on rnd 1, *ch 3, sl st in next unused lp, rep from * around to end of rnd 5. Fasten off.

Stuff.

NOSE
Rnd 1 (RS): With size G hook and 1 strand of petal pink, ch 3, join in first ch to form a ring, ch 1, 2 sc in each ch around. *(6 sc)*

Rnd 2: 2 sc in each sc around. *(12 sc)*

Rnd 3: Sc in each sc around.

Rnd 4: [Sc dec in next 2 sc] 6 times. Leaving a 12-inch end for sewing, fasten off.

EYE
Make 2.
With size G hook and 1 strand of black, ch 2, 7 hdc in 2nd ch from hook, join in top of ch-2. Leaving a 12-inch end for sewing, fasten off.

FINISHING
Note: For following steps, refer to photo for placement.

Step 1: Sew Cheeks to lower half of Head with Cheeks touching at center, stuffing before closing.

Step 2: Positioning dec sts of rnd 23 at center front, flatten Ear. Sew Ears to top of Head 2 inches apart.

Step 3: Sew Tail to center back at bottom of Body.

Step 4: Sew Nose to Head centered at top of Cheeks. Using **straight stitch** *(see Fig. 1)*, with tapestry needle and 2 strands of pink and beg under Nose, work a 1½-inch vertical st between Cheeks.

Fig. 1
Straight Stitch

Step 5: Working in back lps, sew Eyes to Head directly above Cheeks 1½-inches apart.

Step 6: Using straight stitch and pink, embroider 4 long sts over end of each Arm and each Leg.

Step 7: Tie ribbon in bow around neck. ∎

Tiger Cat's Bed

DESIGN BY CYNTHIA HARRIS

SKILL LEVEL
■■□□
EASY

FINISHED SIZE
Approximately 15 inches x 32 inches, excluding tail

MATERIALS
- Red Heart Super Saver medium (worsted) weight yarn (7 oz/364 yds/ 198g per skein):
  2 skeins #312 black
  1 yd #311 white
- Red Heart Classic medium (worsted) weight yarn (3½ oz/190 yds/99g per skein):
  18 skeins #245 orange
- Size K/10½/6.5mm crochet hooks or size needed to obtain gauge
- Tapestry needle
- 1-inch flat black buttons: 2
- 1 yd 1¼-inch-wide pink and white gingham ribbon
- Polyester fiberfill

GAUGE
With 2 strands held tog: 5 sts = 2 inches; 5 rnds = 2 inches

PATTERN NOTES
Tiger is worked in continuous rounds. Do not join unless specified; mark beginning of rounds.

Weave in ends as work progresses.

Join with slip stitch as indicated unless otherwise stated.

Chain-3 at beginning of double crochet rows counts as first double crochet unless otherwise stated.

INSTRUCTIONS
STRIPES
With 2 strands of black, chain amount of chs stated in Stripes Key on page 34, sl st in 2nd ch from hook, sc in next ch, hdc in each rem ch across to last 2 chs, sc in next ch, sl st in last ch. Leaving an 18-inch end for sewing, fasten off.

BODY
Rnd 1 (RS): Starting at front with 2 strands of orange, ch 39, sc in 2nd ch from hook, sc in each of next 36 chs, 2 sc in last ch, working in unused lps on opposite side of starting ch, sc in each of next 37 chs. (*76 sc*)

Rnds 2–51: Sc in each sc around.

Rnd 52: Sc in each sc around, **join** (*see Pattern Notes*) in beg sc. Leaving an 18-inch end for sewing, fasten off.

Stuff with fiberfill.

With tapestry needle and long end, sew opening closed.

Referring to Bed Top Stripes Diagram and Stripes Key on page 34, sew Stripes to Body.

BACK LEG
Make 2.
Rnd 1 (RS): Starting at Paw with 2 strands of orange, ch 3, join in first ch to form a ring, ch 1, 2 sc in each sc around. (*6 sc*)

Rnd 2: 2 sc in each sc around. (*12 sc*)

Rnd 3: [Sc in next sc, 2 sc in next sc] 6 times. (*18 sc*)

Rnd 4: [Sc in each of next 2 sc, 2 sc in next st] 6 times. (*24 sc*)

Rnd 5: [Sc in each of next 3 sc, 2 sc in next sc] 6 times. (*30 sc*)

Rnd 6: [Sc in each of next 4 sc, 2 sc in next st] 6 times. *(36 sc)*

Rnds 7–9: Sc in each sc around.

Rnd 10: [Sc in each of next 4 sc, **sc dec** *(see Stitch Guide)* in next 2 sc] 6 times. *(30 sc)*

Rnd 11: Sc in each sc around.

Rnd 12: [Sc in each of next 3 sc, sc dec in next 2 sc] 6 times. *(24 sc)*

Rnds 13–22: Sc in each sc around.

Rnd 23: [Sc in each of next 3 sc, 2 sc in next sc] 6 times. *(30 sc)*

Rnd 24: [Sc in each of next 4 sc, 2 sc in next st] 6 times. *(36 sc)*

Stuff firmly.

Rnds 25–31: Sc in each sc around.

Rnd 32: [Sc in each of next 4 sc, sc dec in next 2 sc] 6 times. *(30 sc)*

Rnd 33: [Sc in each of next 3 sc, sc dec in next 2 sc] 6 times. *(24 sc)*

Rnd 34: [Sc in each of next 2 sc, sc dec in next 2 sc] 6 times. *(18 sc)*

Stuff lightly.

Rnd 35: [Sc in next sc, sc dec in next 2 sc] 6 times. *(12 sc)*

Rnd 36: [Sl st in next sc, sk next sc] 3 times, join in next sc. Leaving an 18-inch end for sewing, fasten off.

For toes, using **straight stitch** *(see Fig. 1)*, with 1 strand of black, embroider 3 long sts evenly sp over Paw, pulling strand tightly to form slight indentation *(see photo)*.

Fig. 1
Straight Stitch

Referring to Bed Top Stripes Diagram for placement, sew Stripes on Legs. Sew long edge of each Back Leg to back side of Body.

FRONT LEG
Make 2.
Rnds 1–24: Rep rnds 1–24 of Back Leg.

Rnd 25: Sc in each sc around, join in beg sc. Leaving an 18-inch end for sewing, fasten off.

Stuff firmly.

For toes, using straight stitch, with 1 strand of black, embroider 3 long sts evenly sp over Paw, pulling strand tightly to form slight indentation (see photo).

Referring to Bed Top Stripes Diagram for placement, sew Stripes on Legs. Sew long edge of each Front Leg to front end of Body.

HEAD
Make 2.
Rnd 1 (RS): Starting at top with 2 strands of orange, ch 3, join in first ch to form a ring, ch 1, 2 sc in each sc around. (6 sc)

Rnd 2: 2 sc in each sc around. (12 sc)

Rnd 3: [Sc in next sc, 2 sc in next sc] 6 times. (18 sc)

Rnd 4: [Sc in each of next 2 sc, 2 sc in next st] 6 times. (24 sc)

Rnd 5: [Sc in each of next 3 sc, 2 sc in next sc] 6 times. (30 sc)

Rnd 6: [Sc in each of next 4 sc, 2 sc in next st] 6 times. (36 sc)

Rnd 7: [Sc in each of next 5 sc, 2 sc in next sc] 6 times. (42 sc)

Rnd 8: [Sc in each of next 6 sc, 2 sc in next sc] 6 times. (48 sc)

Rnd 8: [Sc in each of next 4 sc, 2 sc in next sc] 6 times. (36 sc)

Rnds 9–22: Sc in each sc around.

Stuff firmly. Continue to stuff as work progresses.

Rnd 23: [Sc in each of next 6 sc, 2 sc in next sc] 6 times. (42 sc)

Rnd 24: [Sc in each of next 5 sc, sc dec in next 2 sc] 6 times. (36 sc)

Rnd 25: [Sc in each of next 4 sc, sc dec in next 2 sc] 6 times. (30 sc)

Rnd 26: [Sc in each of next 3 sc, sc dec in next 2 sc] 6 times. (24 sc)

Rnds 27–29: Sc in each sc around.

Rnd 30: [Sc in each of next 3 sc, 2 sc in next sc] 6 times. (30 sc)

Rnd 31: [Sc in each of next 4 sc, 2 sc in next sc] 6 times. (36 sc)

Rnd 32: Sc in each sc around, join in beg sc. Leaving an 18-inch end for sewing, fasten off.

EAR
Make 2.
Rnd 1 (RS): Starting at top of Head with 2 strands of orange, ch 3, join in first ch to form a ring, ch 1, 2 sc in each sc around. (6 sc)

Rnd 2: 2 sc in each sc around. (12 sc)

Rnd 3: [Sc in next sc, 2 sc in next sc] 6 times. (18 sc)

Rnd 4: [Sc in each of next 2 sc, 2 sc in next st] 6 times. (24 sc)

Rnd 5: [Sc in each of next 3 sc, 2 sc in next sc] 6 times. (30 sc)

Rnd 6: [Sc in each of next 4 sc, 2 sc in next st] 6 times. (36 sc)

Rnd 7: [Sc dec in next 2 sc] 18 times. Leaving a 12-inch end for sewing, fasten off. (18 sc)

Rnd 8: Flatten rnd 7. Working through both thicknesses at same time, sc in each sc across. Leaving an 18-inch end for sewing, fasten off.

Sew straight edge of each Ear to top of Head
3 inches apart *(see photo).*

MUZZLE
Rnd 1 (RS): With 2 strands of orange, ch 3, join
in first ch to form a ring, ch 1, 2 sc in each sc
around. *(6 sc)*

Rnd 2: 2 sc in each sc around. *(12 sc)*

Rnd 3: [Sc in next sc, 2 sc in next sc]
6 times. *(18 sc)*

Rnd 4: [Sc in each of next 2 sc, 2 sc in next st]
6 times. *(24 sc)*

Rnd 5: [Sc in each of next 3 sc, 2 sc in next sc]
6 times. *(30 sc)*

Rnd 6: [Sc in each of next 4 sc, 2 sc in next st]
6 times. *(36 sc)*

Rnd 7: [Sc in each of next 5 sc, 2 sc in next st]
6 times. *(42 sc)*

Rnds 8–10: Sc in each sc around.

Rnd 11: Sc in each sc around, join in beg sc.
Leaving an 18-inch end for sewing, fasten off.

Sew Muzzle centered over rnds 16–28 on
lower half of Head, stuffing before closing
(see photo).

CHEEK
Make 2.
Rnd 1 (RS): With 2 strands of orange, ch 3, join
in first ch to form a ring, ch 1, 2 sc in each sc
around. *(6 sc)*

Rnd 2: 2 sc in each sc around. *(12 sc)*

Rnd 3: [Sc in next sc, 2 sc in next sc]
6 times. *(18 sc)*

Rnd 4: [Sc in each of next 2 sc, 2 sc in next st]
6 times. *(24 sc)*

Rnd 5: Sc in each sc around.

Rnd 6: Sc in each sc around, join in first sc.
Leaving an 18-inch end for sewing, fasten off.

Sew Cheeks to Muzzle, stuffing before closing.

TAIL
Rnd 1 (RS): With 2 strands of orange, ch 3, join
in first ch to form a ring, ch 1, 2 sc in each sc
around. *(6 sc)*

Rnd 2: 2 sc in each sc around. *(12 sc)*

Rnd 3: [Sc in each of next 2 sc, 2 sc in next sc]
4 times. *(16 sc)*

Stuff lightly. Continue to stuff as work
progresses.

Rnds 4–35: Sc in each sc around.

Rnd 36: [Sc in each of next 3 sc, 2 sc in next sc]
4 times. *(20 sc)*

Rnds 37 & 38: Sc in each sc around.

Rnd 39: [Sc in each of next 4 sc, 2 sc in next sc]
4 times. *(24 sc)*

Rnd 40: Sc in each sc around, join in beg sc.
Leaving an 18-inch end for sewing,
fasten off.

NOSE
Make 2.
Row 1 (RS): With 2 strands of black, ch 2,
2 sc in 2nd ch from hook, turn. *(2 sc)*

Row 2: Ch 1, 2 sc in each sc, turn. *(4 sc)*

Row 3: Ch 1, 2 sc in first sc, sc in each of next
2 sc, 2 sc in last sc. Leaving a 12-inch end for
sewing, fasten off. *(6 sc)*

Note: Row 3 is top of Nose.

Sew Nose to Muzzle centered between Cheeks,
stuffing lightly before closing.

FINISHING
*Note: For following steps, refer to Head Stripes
Diagram and photo for placement.*

Step 1: Using straight stitch with 1 strand of
black, embroider 2 long sts between Cheeks
at center bottom of Nose.

Step 2: For eyes, using **satin stitch** *(see Fig. 2)*, with 1 strand of white, embroider sts over rnd 15 of Head directly above Muzzle 2 inches apart.

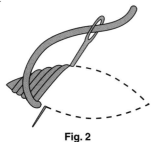

Fig. 2
Satin Stitch

Step 3: For pupil, using satin stitch, with 1 strand of black, embroider sts centered vertically over white of eye.

Step 4: Center and sew Head to top of front of Body with Head turned slightly towards the left Front Leg.

Step 5: Sew Stripes to Head.

Step 6: Sew Tail to center back of Body. Sew Stripes to Tail, with 6 Stripes down 1 side of Tail and 5 Stripes down other side.

Step 7: With 1 strand of orange and going through all thicknesses, sew 1 button centered on top of Body 7 inches from Tail; center and sew other button 8 inches from first button *(see Bed Top Stripes Diagram)*. ■

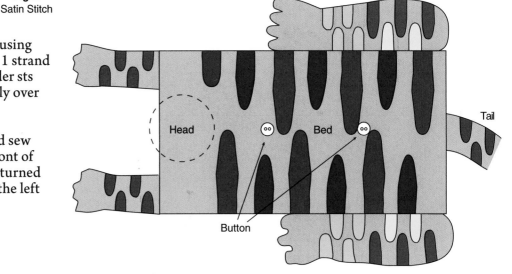

Tiger Cat's Bed
Bed Top Stripes Diagram

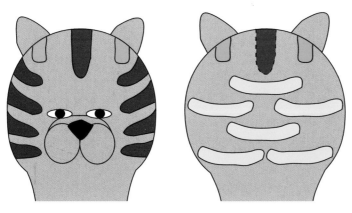

Tiger Cat's Bed
Head Stripes Diagram

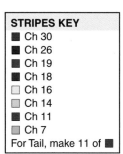

STRIPES KEY
- Ch 30
- Ch 26
- Ch 19
- Ch 18
- Ch 16
- Ch 14
- Ch 11
- Ch 7
- For Tail, make 11 of ■

Reginald & Regina

DESIGNS BY
ROBIN L. MURPHY

Elephant

SKILL LEVEL

EASY

FINISHED SIZE

Approximately 14½ inches tall

MATERIALS

- Medium (worsted) weight yarn:
  9½ oz/475 yds/269g white
  7 oz/350 yds/198g gray
  3½ oz/175 yds/99g each light pink
  and dark pink
  2 oz/100 yds/56g blue

- Sizes F/5/3.75mm and G/6/4mm crochet
  hooks or sizes needed to obtain gauge
- Tapestry needle
- Sewing needle
- 4 black 15mm shank-back buttons
- 5 white ½-inch buttons
- 5 white ⅛-inch buttons
- Fiberfill
- Sewing thread

GAUGE

Size F hook: 5 sc = 1 inch; 5 sc rows = 1 inch

Size G hook: 4 dc = 1 inch; 2 dc rnds = 1 inch

PATTERN NOTES

Elephant is worked in continuous rounds. Do not join unless specified; mark beginning of rounds.

Weave in ends as work progresses.

Join with slip stitch as indicated unless otherwise stated.

For the safety of children under 3 years, do not use shank-back button eyes, animal noses or decorative buttons. Instead, with crochet hook size C, crochet small (5 sc) circles.

Chain-3 at beginning of rows counts as first double crochet unless otherwise stated.

INSTRUCTIONS
REGINALD ELEPHANT
HEAD

Rnd 1 (RS): Beg with trunk with size F hook and gray, ch 2, 6 sc in 2nd ch from hook. *(6 sc)*

Rnd 2: [Sc in next sc, 2 sc in next sc] 3 times. *(9 sc)*

Rnd 3: Ch 1, sc in each sc around, **join** *(see Pattern Notes)* in beg sc.

Rnd 4: Rep rnd 3.

Rnd 5: Ch 1, [sc in each of next 2 sc, 2 sc in next sc] 3 times, join in beg sc. *(12 sc)*

Rnd 6: Rep rnd 3.

Rnd 7: Ch 1, [sc in each of next 3 sc, 2 sc in next sc] 3 times, join in beg sc. *(15 sc)*

Rnd 8: Ch 1, sc in each of next 5 sc, sl st loosely in each of next 5 sc, sc in each of next 5 sc, join in beg sc.

Rnd 9: Ch 1, hdc in each of next 4 sts, sc in next st, sl st loosely in each of next 5 sts, sc in next st, hdc in each of next 4 sts, join in beg hdc.

Rnd 10: Ch 1, [sc in each of next 4 sts, 2 sc in next st] 3 times, join in beg sc. *(18 sc)*

Rnd 11: Rep rnd 3.

Rnd 12: Ch 1, [sc in each of next 5 sc, 2 sc in next sc] 3 times, join in beg sc. *(21 sc)*

Rnd 13: Rep rnd 3.

Rnd 14: [Sc in each of next 6 sc, 2 sc in next sc] 3 times. *(24 sc)*

Rnd 15: Rep rnd 3.

Rnd 16: Ch 1, [sc in each of next 3 sc, 2 sc in next sc] 6 times, join in beg sc. *(30 sc)*

Rnd 17: Ch 1, [sc in each of next 4 sc, 2 sc in next sc] 6 times, join in beg sc. *(36 sc)*

Rnd 18: Ch 1, [sc in each of next 5 sc, 2 sc in next sc] 6 times, join in beg sc. *(42 sc)*

Rnd 19: Ch 1, sc in each of next 9 sc, 2 sc in each of next 3 sc, sc in each of next 21 sc, 2 sc in each of next 3 sc, sc in each of next 6 sc, join in beg sc. *(48 sc)*

Rnd 20: Ch 1, sc in each of next 8 sc, [2 sc in next sc, sc in each of next 2 sc] twice, 2 sc in next sc, sc in each of next 19 sc, [2 sc in next sc, sc in each of next 2 sc] twice, 2 sc in next sc, sc in each of next 7 sc, join in beg sc. *(54 sc)*

Rnd 21: Rep rnd 3.

Rnd 22: Ch 1, sc in each of next 10 sc, [**sc dec** *(see Stitch Guide)* in next 2 sc] 6 times, 2 sc in next sc, 2 hdc in each of next 12 sc, 2 sc in next sc, [sc dec in next 2 sc] 6 times, sc in each of next 6 sc, join in beg sc. *(56 sts)*

Rnd 23: Ch 1, sc in each of next 8 sts, [sc dec in next 2 sts] 4 times, 2 sc in next st, sc in each of next 25 sts, 2 sc in next st, [sc dec in next 2 sts] 4 times, sc in each of next 5 sts, join in beg sc. *(50 sts)*

Rnd 24: Ch 1, sl st loosely in each of next 7 sts, hdc in each of next 5 sts, 2 sc in next st, sc in each of next 27 sts, 2 sc in next st, hdc in each of next 5 sts, leaving rem 4 sts unworked, loosely ch 11 *(neck opening)*, join in beg hdc. Fasten off. *(41 sts)*

Rnd 25: Join gray in 6th ch of ch-11, ch 1, sc in same ch as joining, sc in each of next 5 chs, sc in each of next 4 sts, 2 sc in each of next 2 sts, sc in each of next 30 sts, 2 sc in each of next 2 sts, sc in each of next 3 sts, sc in each of next 5 chs, join in beg sc. *(56 sc)*

Rnd 26: Rep rnd 3.

Rnd 27: Ch 1, sc in each of next 6 sc, sc dec in next 2 sc, sc in each of next 42 sc, sc dec in next 2 sc, sc in each of next 4 sc, join in beg sc. *(54 sc)*

Rnd 28: Ch 1, [sc dec in next 2 sc, sc in each of next 7 sc] 6 times, join in beg sc dec. *(48 sc)*

Sew 15mm black shank-back buttons 12 sc apart between rnds 21 and 22 above cheeks.

Leaving rnds 1–8 of trunk unstuffed, stuff rem of trunk and head firmly with fiberfill, shaping as work progresses.

Rnd 29: Ch 1, [sc in each of next 6 sc, sc dec in next 2 sc] 6 times, join in beg sc. *(42 sc)*

Rnd 30: Ch 1, [sc dec in next 2 sc, sc in each of next 5 sc] 6 times, join in beg sc. *(36 sc)*

Rnd 31: Ch 1, [sc in each of next 4 sc, sc dec in next 2 sc] 6 times, join in beg sc. *(30 sc)*

Rnd 32: Ch 1, [sc dec in next 2 sc, sc in each of next 3 sc] 6 times, join in beg sc. *(24 sc)*

Stuff firmly with fiberfill; continue stuffing and shaping as work progresses.

Rnd 33: Ch 1, [sc in each of next 2 sc, sc dec in next 2 sc] 6 times, join in beg sc. *(18 sc)*

Rnd 34: Ch 1, [sc dec in next 2 sc, sc in next sc] 6 times, join in beg sc. *(12 sc)*

Rnd 35: Ch 1, [sc dec in next 2 sc] 6 times, join in beg sc. Leaving a 12-inch end for sewing, fasten off. *(6 sc)*

With tapestry needle, sew opening closed.

BOTTOM LIP

Rnd 1 (RS): With size F hook and gray, ch 2, 8 sc in 2nd ch from hook, join in beg sc. *(8 sc)*

Rnd 2: Ch 1, sc in each sc around, join in beg sc.

Rnd 3: Ch 1, [sc in next sc, 2 sc in next sc] 4 times, join in beg sc. *(12 sc)*

Rnd 4: Ch 1, sc in each sc around, join in beg sc. Leaving a 12-inch end for sewing, fasten off.

With tapestry needle, sew below trunk across rnd 15.

BODY

Rnd 1 (RS): Working in sts on rnd 24 of Head, with size F hook, join gray in 6th ch of ch-11, ch 1, sc in same ch as joining, work 23 sc evenly sp around, join in beg sc. *(24 sc)*

Rnd 2: Ch 1, sc in each sc around, join in beg sc.

Rnd 3: Ch 1, [sc in each of next 3 sc, 2 sc in next sc] 6 times, join in beg sc. *(30 sc)*

Rnd 4: Rep rnd 2.

Rnd 5: Ch 1, [sc in each of next 4 sc, 2 sc in next sc] 6 times, join in beg sc. *(36 sc)*

Rnd 6: Rep rnd 2.

Rnd 7: Ch 1, [sc in each of next 5 sc, 2 sc in next sc] 6 times, join in beg sc. *(42 sc)*

Rnd 8: Rep rnd 2.

Rnd 9: Ch 1, sc in each of next 14 sc, 2 sc in each of next 3 sc, sc in each of next 5 sc, 2 sc in each of next 3 sc, sc in each of next 17 sc, join in beg sc. *(48 sc)*

Rnd 10: Rep rnd 2.

Rnd 11: Ch 1, sc in each of next 15 sc, [sc dec in next 2 sc] 3 times, sc in each of next 3 sc, [sc dec in next 2 sc] 3 times, sc in each of next 18 sc, join in beg sc. *(42 sc)*

Rnd 12: Ch 1, [sc in each of next 6 sc, 2 sc in next sc] 6 times, join in beg sc. *(48 sc)*

Rnd 13: Rep rnd 2.

Rnd 14: Ch 1, [sc in each of next 7 sc, 2 sc in next sc] 6 times, join in beg sc. *(54 sc)*

Rnd 15: Ch 1, [sc in each of next 8 sc, 2 sc in next sc] 6 times, join in beg sc. *(60 sc)*

Rnd 16: Rep rnd 2.

Rnd 17: Ch 1, [sc in each of next 8 sc, sc dec in next 2 sc] 6 times, join in beg sc. *(54 sc)*

Rnd 18: Rep rnd 2.

Rnd 19: Ch 1, [sc in each of next 7 sc, sc dec in next 2 sc] 6 times, join in beg sc. *(48 sc)*

Stuff firmly; continue stuffing and shaping as work progresses.

Rnds 20–26: Rep rnds 29–35 of Head.

With tapestry needle, sew opening closed.

EAR
Make 2.
Row 1 (RS): With size F hook and gray, ch 9, sc in 2nd ch from hook, sc in each rem ch across, turn. *(8 sc)*

Row 2: Ch 1, 2 sc in first sc, sc in each sc across to last sc, 2 sc in last sc, turn. *(10 sc)*

Rows 3–5: Rep row 3. *(16 sc at end of last row)*

Row 6: Ch 1, sc in each sc across, turn.

Row 7: Ch 1, sc dec in first 2 sc, sc in each sc across to last 2 sc, sc dec in last 2 sc, turn. *(14 sc)*

Rows 8–10: Rep row 7. *(8 sc at end of last row)*

Row 11: Ch 1, sc dec in first 2 sc, sc in each of next 4 sc, sc dec in last 2 sc. *(6 sc)*

EDGING
Row 1 (RS): Ch 1, working across next side in ends of rows, work 11 sc evenly sp across side, working across next side in unused lps of beg ch, work 8 sc evenly sp across, working across next side in ends of rows, work 11 sc evenly sp across side edge of rows, **do not work across sts of row 11**. *(30 sc)*

Rnd 2: Ch 1, working left to right, work **reverse sc** *(see Fig. 1)* in each sc around to beg reverse sc, join in beg reverse sc. Leaving a 12-inch end for sewing, fasten off.

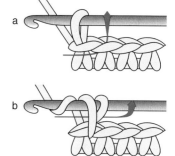

Fig. 1
Reverse Single Crochet

With tapestry needle, sew Ears to rnd 27 of Head, having 14 sc between Ears.

LEG
Make 2.
Rnd 1 (RS): With size F hook and gray, ch 2, 8 sc in 2nd ch from hook, join in beg sc. *(8 sc)*

Rnd 2: Ch 1, 2 sc in each sc around, join in beg sc. *(16 sc)*

Rnd 3: Rep rnd 2. *(32 sc)*

Rnd 4: Ch 1, sc in each sc around, join in beg sc.

Rnd 5: Ch 1, [sc in each of next 7 sc, 2 sc in next sc] 4 times, join in **back lp** *(see Stitch Guide)* of beg sc. *(36 sc)*

Rnd 6: Ch 1, working in back lps only, sc in each of next 14 sc, [sc dec in next 2 sc] 4 times *(center front of foot)*, sc in each of next 14 sc, join in beg sc. *(32 sc)*

Rnd 7: Ch 1, sc in each of next 12 sc, [sc dec in next 2 sc] 4 times, sc in each of next 12 sc, join in beg sc. *(28 sc)*

Rnd 8: Ch 1, sc dec in next 2 sc, sc in each of next 5 sc, sc dec in next 2 sc, sc in each of next 3 sc, [sc dec in next 2 sc] twice, sc in each of next 3 sc, sc dec in next 2 sc, sc in each of next 5 sc, sc dec in next 2 sc, join in beg sc. *(22 sc)*

Rnd 9: Ch 1, [sc in each of next 3 sc, sc dec in next 2 sc] 4 times, sc in each of next 2 sc, join in beg sc. *(18 sc)*

Rnds 10–19: Rep rnd 4.

Rnd 20: Ch 1, sc in each of next 9 sc, 2 sc in each of next 4 sc, sc in each of next 5 sc, join in beg sc. *(22 sc)*

Rnds 21–23: Rep rnd 4.

Rnd 24: Ch 1, sc in each of next 9 sc, [sc dec in next 2 sc] 4 times, sc in each of next 5 sc, join in beg sc. *(18 sc)*

Rnds 25–31: Rep rnd 4.

Stuff firmly.

Row 32: Flatten rnd 31, ch 1, now working in a row and working through both thicknesses at same time, sc in each of next 9 sc. Leaving a 12-inch end for sewing, fasten off.

With tapestry needle, sew Legs to bottom of Body.

ARM
Make 2.
Rnd 1 (RS): With size F hook, ch 2, 8 sc in 2nd ch from hook, join in beg sc. *(8 sc)*

Rnd 2: Ch 1, 2 sc in each sc around, join in beg sc. *(16 sc)*

Rnd 3: Ch 1, [sc in next sc, 2 sc in next sc] 8 times, join in beg sc. *(24 sc)*

Rnd 4: Ch 1, sc in each sc around, join in beg sc.

Rnds 5 & 6: Rep rnd 4.

Rnd 7: Ch 1, sc in each of next 10 sc, sc dec in next 4 sc, sc in each of next 10 sc, join in beg sc. *(21 sc)*

Rnd 8: Ch 1, sc dec in next 2 sc, sc in each of next 7 sc, sc dec in next 4 sc, sc in each of next 6 sc, sc dec in next 2 sc, join in beg sc dec. *(16 sc)*

Rnd 9: Rep rnd 4.

Rnd 10: Ch 1, sc in each of next 8 sc, sc dec in next 2 sc, sc in each of next 6 sc, join in beg sc. *(15 sc)*

Rnds 11–13: Rep rnd 4.

Rnd 14: Ch 1, 2 hdc in first sc, sc in each of next 6 sc, sl st loosely in each of next 3 sc, sc in each of next 4 sc, 2 hdc in next sc, join in beg hdc. *(17 sts)*

Rnd 15: Ch 1, hdc in each of next 2 sts, sc in each of next 6 sts, sl st loosely in each of next 3 sts, sc in each of next 4 sts, hdc in each of next 2 sts, join in beg hdc.

Rnd 16: Ch 1, sc dec in next 2 sts, sc in each of next 6 sc, sc in each of next 3 sl sts, sc in each of next 4 sc, sc dec in next 2 sts, join in beg sc. *(15 sc)*

Rnds 17–24: Rep rnd 4.

Stuff firmly.

Row 25: Flatten rnd 24, ch 1, now working in a row and working through both thicknesses at same time, work 8 sc evenly spaced across. Leaving a 12-inch end for sewing, fasten off.

With tapestry needle, sew Arms to side of Body over rnd 5.

VEST
Row 1 (RS): With size G hook and blue, ch 26, sc in 2nd ch from hook, sc in each rem ch across, turn. *(25 sc)*

Row 2: Ch 1, sc in each of first 3 sc, 2 sc in each of next 19 sc, sc in each of next 3 sc, turn. *(44 sc)*

Row 3: Ch 1, sc in each of first 3 sc, 2 sc in next sc, [sc in each of next 3 sc, 2 sc in next sc] 9 times, sc in each of next 4 sc, turn. *(54 sc)*

Row 4: Ch 1, sc in each sc across, turn.

Row 5: Ch 1, sc in each of next 5 sc, ch 9 *(armhole opening)*, sk next 15 sc, sc in each of next 14 sc, ch 9 *(armhole opening)*, sk next 15 sc, sc in each of next 5 sc, turn. *(24 sc, 2 ch-9 sps)*

Row 6: Ch 1, sc in each sc and each ch across, turn. *(42 sc)*

Rows 7–12: Rep row 4. At end of row 12, do not turn.

BUTTONHOLE BAND

Row 1: Ch 1, working across next side in ends of rows, work 12 sc evenly sp across, turn. *(12 sc)*

Row 2: Ch 1, sc in each of first 12 sc, turn.

Row 3: Ch 1, sc in first sc, [ch 1 *(buttonhole)*, sk next 2 sc, sc in each of next 2 sc] twice, ch 1 *(buttonhole)*, sk next 2 sc, sc in last sc, turn.

Row 4: Ch 1, sc in first sc, [2 sc in next ch-1 sp, sc in each of next 2 sc] twice, 2 sc in next ch-1 sp, sc in next sc. Fasten off. *(12 sc)*

BUTTON BAND

Row 1 (RS): Beg at neckline edge and with size G hook, join blue in end of row 1 of left front, ch 1, work 12 sc evenly sp across, turn. *(12 sc)*

Rows 2–4: Ch 1, sc in each of next 12 sc, turn. At end of row 4, fasten off.

COLLAR

Row 1 (RS): Sk rows 2–4 of Buttonhole Band, with size G hook, join blue in end of row 1 of Buttonhole Band, ch 1, sc in same sp, working in unused lps on opposite side of beg ch, sc in each of next 25 chs, sc in row 1 of Button Band, turn. *(27 sc)*

Row 2: Ch 1, sc dec in first 2 sc, sc in each of next 23 sc, sc dec in last 2 sc, turn. *(25 sc)*

Row 3: Ch 1, sc dec in first 2 sc, sc in each of next 21 sc, sc dec in last 2 sc. *(23 sc)*

EDGING

Ch 1, working left to right, work reverse sc in each st evenly sp around entire outer edge of piece, join in beg reverse sc. Fasten off.

ARMHOLE TRIM

With RS facing and with size G hook, join blue in 1 underarm section, ch 1, working left to right, work reverse sc evenly sp around armhole opening, join in beg reverse sc. Fasten off.

FINISHING

With sewing needle and matching thread, sew 3½-inch white buttons on Button Band opposite buttonholes.

PANTS

Rnd 1 (RS): With size G hook and white, ch 50, join in first ch to form a ring, ch 1, sc in each ch around, join in beg sc. *(50 sc)*

Rnd 2: Ch 3 *(see Pattern Notes)*, dc in each of next 2 sc, working in **back lps** *(see Stitch Guide)* only, dc in each of next 4 sc, working through both lps, dc in each of next 36 sc, working in back lps only, dc in each of next 4 sc, working through both lps, dc in each of next 3 sc, join in 3rd ch of beg ch-3.

Rnd 3: Ch 3, dc in same ch as joining, dc in each rem dc around, join in 3rd ch of beg ch-3. *(51 dc)*

Rnd 4: Ch 3, dc in each dc around, join in 3rd ch of beg ch-3.

Rnds 5 & 6: Rep rnd 4.

FIRST LEG

Rnd 7: Ch 3, sk next 25 dc, sl st in next dc, ch 3, dc in each rem dc around, dc in each of next 3 chs, join in 3rd ch of beg ch-3. *(28 dc)*

Rnds 8 & 9: Rep rnd 4. At end of rnd 9, fasten off.

2ND LEG

Rnd 7: With size G hook, join white in next unused dc of rnd 6 at back, ch 3, dc in each rem dc around, dc in each of next 3 chs, join in 3rd ch of beg ch-3. *(28 dc)*

Rnds 8 & 9: Rep rnds 8 and 9 of First Leg.

WAISTBAND

Rnd 1 (RS): With RS facing and working in unused lps on opposite side of starting ch, with size G hook, join white at back of Pants, ch 1, sc in each ch around, join in beg sc. *(50 sc)*

Rnd 2: Ch 1, working left to right, work reverse sc in each sc around, join in beg reverse sc. Fasten off.

SHOULDER STRAP
Make 2.
Row 1 (RS): Working in rem 4 unused lps of rnd 1 at back, with size G hook, join white in first unused lp, ch 1, sc in same sp, sc in each of next 3 lps, turn. *(4 sc)*

Rows 2–22: Ch 1, sc in each sc, turn.

Row 23: Ch 1, sc in first sc, ch 1 *(buttonhole)*, sk next 2 sc, sc in last sc, turn.

Row 24: Ch 1, sc in first sc, 2 sc in next ch-1 sp, sc in last sc. Fasten off. *(4 sc)*

FINISHING
Place Pants on elephant. With sewing needle and matching thread, sew rem 2 ⅛-inch white buttons on waistband front to correspond with ends of straps. Place Vest on elephant.

REGINA ELEPHANT
With white, work same as Reginald Elephant through Arm.

PANTIES
Rnd 1 (RS): With size G hook and light pink, ch 50, join in first ch to form a ring, ch 1, sc in each ch around, join in beg sc. *(50 sc)*

Rnd 2: Ch 1, working in back lps only, sc in each sc around, join in beg sc.

Rnd 3: Ch 3 *(see Pattern Notes)*, dc in same sc as joining, [dc in each of next 2 sc, 2 dc in next sc] 16 times, dc in next sc, join in 3rd ch of beg ch-3. *(67 dc)*

Rnds 4–6: Ch 3, dc in each st around, join in 3rd ch of beg ch-3.

FIRST LEG
Rnd 7: Ch 3, sk next 33 dc, sl st in next dc, ch 3, dc in each dc and each ch around, join in 3rd ch of beg ch-3. *(36 dc)*

Rnd 8: Ch 3, dc in each of next 3 dc, sc dec in next 2 dc, [dc in each of next 4 dc, sc dec in next 2 dc] 5 times, join in 3rd ch of beg ch-3. *(30 dc)*

Rnd 9: Ch 1, sc in each st around, join in beg sc.

Rnd 10: Ch 1, working left to right, work reverse sc in each sc around, join in beg reverse sc. Fasten off.

2ND LEG
Rnd 7: Beg at back and with size G hook, join light pink in next unused dc of rnd 6, ch 3, dc in each dc and each ch around, join in 3rd ch of beg ch-3. *(36 dc)*

Rnds 8–10: Rep rnds 8–10 of First Leg.

BODICE
Row 1 (RS): With size G hook and light pink, ch 4 *(buttonhole extension)*, working in unused lps on opposite side of starting ch of Panties, sc in each lp around, turn. *(4 chs, 50 sc)*

Row 2: Ch 1, sc in each of next 50 sc, sc in each of next 4 chs, turn. *(54 sc)*

Row 3: Ch 1, sc in each of next 2 sc, ch 1 *(buttonhole)*, sk next 2 sc, sc in each sc across, turn.

Row 4: Ch 1, sc in each of next 50 sc, 2 sc in next ch-1 sp, sc in each of next 2 sc, turn. *(54 sc)*

Row 5: Ch 1, sc in each of next 2 sc, ch 1 *(buttonhole)*, sk next 2 sc, sc in each of next 8 sc, ch 18 *(armhole opening)*, sk next 8 sc, sc in each of next 20 sc, ch 18 *(armhole opening)*, sk next 8 sc, sc in each of next 6 sc, turn.

Row 6: Ch 1, sc in each of next 6 sc, sc in each of next 18 chs, sc in each of next 20 sc, sc in each of next 18 chs, sc in each of next 8 sc, 2 sc in ch-1 sp, sc in each of next 2 sc, turn. *(74 sc)*

Row 7: Ch 1, sc in each of next 2 sc, ch 1 *(buttonhole)*, sk next 2 sc, sc in each of next 4 sc, [sc dec in next 2 sc] 13 times, sc in each of next 12 sc, [sc dec in next 2 sc] 13 times, sc in each of next 2 sc, turn. *(46 sc, 1 ch-1 sp)*

Row 8: Ch 1, sc in each of next 44 sc, 2 sc in next ch-1 sp, sc in each of next 2 sc, turn. *(48 sc)*

Row 9: Ch 1, sc in each of next 2 sc, ch 1 *(buttonhole)*, sk next 2 sc, sc in each of next 3 sc, [sc dec in next 2 sc] twice, sc in each of next 8 sc, [sc dec in next 2 sc] twice, sc in each of next

9 sc, [sc dec in next 2 sc] twice, sc in each of next 8 sc, sc dec in next 2 sc, sc in each of next 2 sc, turn.

Row 10: Ch 1, sc in each of next 37 sc, 2 sc in next ch-1 sp, sc in each of next 2 sc. Fasten off. *(41 sc)*

Sew 4⅛-inch white buttons down back opening to correspond with buttonholes.

Sew ⅛-inch white button at center front of Bodice neckline.

SLEEVE
Make 2.
Rnd 1 (RS): With size G hook, join light pink in 4th sc of 1 underarm section, ch 1, 26 sc evenly sp around armhole opening, join in beg sc. *(26 sc)*

Rnd 2: Ch 1, sc in same sc as joining, [ch 4, sc in next sc] 25 times, ch 2, join with hdc in beg sc.

Rnd 3: Ch 1, sc in sp formed by joining hdc, *ch 3, sc in next ch-4 sp, rep from * around, ch 1, join with hdc in beg sc.

Rnd 4: Ch 1, sc in sp formed by joining hdc, sc in each rem ch-3 sp around, join in beg sc. *(26 sc)*

Rnd 5: Ch 1, [sc in each of next 3 sc, sc dec in next 2 sc] 5 times, sc in last sc, join in beg sc. Fasten off. *(21 sc)*

SKIRT
Rnd 1 (RS): With size G hook, join dark pink in first unused lp at back of rnd 1 of Panties, ch 3, dc in same lp, 2 dc in each rem lp around, join in 3rd ch of beg ch-3. *(100 dc)*

Rnds 2–10: Ch 3, dc in each dc around, join in 3rd ch of beg ch-3.

Rnd 11: Ch 1, working left to right, work reverse sc in each dc around, join in beg reverse sc. Fasten off.

HEADBAND
BOW
Row 1 (RS): With size G hook and dark pink, ch 6, sc in 2nd ch from hook, sc in each rem ch across, turn. *(5 sc)*

Row 2: Ch 1, sc in each sc across, turn.

Row 3: Ch 1, sc dec in first 2 sc, sc in next sc, sc dec in next 2 sc, turn. *(3 sc)*

Row 4: Ch 1, working in back lps only, sc dec in first 3 sc, turn. *(1 sc)*

Row 5: Ch 1, 3 sc in sc, turn. *(3 sc)*

Row 6: Ch 1, working in back lps only, ch 1, 2 sc in first sc, sc in next sc, 2 sc in last sc, turn. *(5 sc)*

Rows 7 & 8: Rep row 2.

EDGING
Ch 1, working left to right, work reverse sc evenly sp around entire outer edge, join in beg reverse sc. Fasten off.

FIRST TIE
Row 1 (RS): With size G hook, join dark pink in first unused lp on row 3, ch 1, sc in same lp, sc in each of next 2 lps, turn. *(3 sc)*

Rows 2–14: Ch 1, sc in each sc across, turn. *(3 sc)*

Row 15: Ch 1, sc dec in first 3 sc, ch 15. Fasten off.

2ND TIE
Row 1 (RS): With size G hook, join dark pink in first unused lp on row 5, ch 1, sc in same lp, sc in each of next 2 lps, turn. *(3 sc)*

Rows 2–15: Rep rows 2–15 of First Tie.

FINISHING
Place Dress on elephant. Referring to photo for placement, tie Headband around Head. ∎

Unicorn Doorstop

DESIGN BY CYNTHIA HARRIS

SKILL LEVEL

EASY

FINISHED SIZE
Approximately 24 inches tall

MATERIALS
- Red Heart Super Saver medium (worsted) weight yarn (7 oz/364 yds/ 198g per skein):
  - 3 skeins #311 white
  - 1 skein #358 lavender
- Size K/10½/6.5mm crochet hook or size needed to obtain gauge
- Tapestry needle
- 1½ yds lavender with gold wire-edged 1½-inch wide ribbon
- 4 yds gold holographic ¼-inch wide rickrack trim
- 24 metallic gold 1 inch x 1¼ inch ribbon bows with rosebud centers
- Scrap pieces of black and white felt
- Minimum 5 lbs dried beans or sand
- 1 clean and dry plastic gallon milk jug with lid
- Fiberfill
- Craft glue

GAUGE
With 2 strands held tog: 3 sts = 1¼ inches; 3 sc rnds = 1¼ inches

PATTERN NOTES
Unicorn is worked in continuous rnds. Do not join unless specified; mark beginning of rounds.

Weave in ends as work progresses.

Join with slip stitch as indicated unless otherwise stated.

Chain-2 at beginning of rows counts as first half double crochet unless otherwise stated.

INSTRUCTIONS
BODY
Rnd 1 (RS): Beg at bottom with 2 strands of white, ch 3, **join** (see Pattern Notes) in first ch to form a ring, ch 1, 2 sc in each ch around. (6 sc)

Rnd 2: 2 sc in each sc around. (12 sc)

Rnd 3: 2 sc in each sc around. (24 sc)

Rnd 4: [Sc in each of next 2 sc, 2 sc in next sc] 8 times. (32 sc)

Rnd 5: [Sc in each of next 3 sc, 2 sc in next sc] 8 times. (40 sc)

Rnd 6: [Sc in each of next 4 sc, 2 sc in next sc] 8 times. (48 sc)

Rnds 7–30: Sc in each sc around.

Place plastic jug inside of Body. Stuff around sides and in front of jug. Handle will be at the center back of Body. (*Do not stuff too full; sts should not be stretched in front. Body should fit smoothly over back of jug.*)

Rnd 31: [Sc in each of next 4 sc, **sc dec** (*see Stitch Guide*) in next 2 sc] 8 times. *(40 sc)*

Rnd 32: Sc in each sc around.

Rnd 33: [Sc in each of next 3 sc, sc dec in next 2 sc] 8 times. *(32 sc)*

Rnd 34: Rep rnd 32.

Rnd 35: [Sc in each of next 2 sc, sc dec in next 2 sc] 8 times. *(24 sc)*

Rnd 36: [Sc dec in next 2 sc] 12 times. *(12 sc)*

Rnd 37: [Sc dec in next 2 sc] 6 times, join in first sc. Fasten off. *(6 sc)*

Note: Top of Body does not have to be sewn together; the Head will cover this area.

Fill jug with dried beans or sand. Place lid on jug, secure or glue in place.

HANDLE
Thread tapestry needle with 2 strands of green; press Body tog through opening of jug handle and sew sides that have been pressed tog, stitching back and forth through opening (*see Milk Jug Diagram*).

Sew sides of Body together.

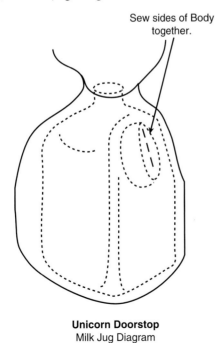

Unicorn Doorstop
Milk Jug Diagram

HEAD
Rnd 1 (RS): Beg at top with 2 strands of white, ch 3, join in first ch to form a ring, ch 1, 2 sc in each ch around. *(6 sc)*

Rnd 2: 2 sc in each sc around. *(12 sc)*

Rnd 3: [Sc in next sc, 2 sc in next sc] 6 times. *(18 sc)*

Rnd 4: [Sc in each of next 2 sc, 2 sc in next sc] 6 times. *(24 sc)*

Rnd 5: [Sc in each of next 3 sc, 2 sc in next sc] 6 times. *(30 sc)*

Rnd 6: [Sc in each of next 4 sc, 2 sc in next sc] 6 times. *(36 sc)*

Rnd 7: [Sc in each of next 5 sc, 2 sc in next sc] 6 times. *(42 sc)*

Rnds 8–14: Sc in each sc around.

Rnd 15: [Sc in each of next 6 sc, 2 sc in next sc] 6 times. *(48 sc)*

Rnds 16–18: Sc in each sc around.

Rnd 19: [Sc in each of next 6 sc, **sc dec** (*see Stitch Guide*) in next 2 sc] 6 times. *(42 sc)*

Rnd 20: [Sc in each of next 5 sc, sc dec in next 2 sc] 6 times. *(36 sc)*

Rnd 21: [Sc in each of next 4 sc, sc dec in next 2 sc] 6 times. *(30 sc)*

Rnd 22: [Sc in each of next 3 sc, sc dec in next 2 sc] 6 times. *(24 sc)*

Rnd 23: Sc in each sc around.

Rnd 24: Sc in each sc around, join in first sc. Leaving a 28-inch end for sewing, fasten off.

Stuff Head firmly with fiberfill, leaving a small opening in center bottom of Head to allow room for top of jug.

Sew Head to rnd 35 of Body.

LEG

Make 2.

Rnd 1 (RS): With 2 strands of lavender, ch 7, 2 sc in 2nd ch from hook, sc in each of next 4 chs, 4 sc in last ch, working in unused lps on opposite side of beg ch, sc in each of next 4 chs, 2 sc in next ch. (*16 sc*)

Rnd 2: 2 sc in each of next 2 sc, sc in each of next 4 sc, 2 sc in each of next 4 sc, sc in each of next 4 sc, 2 sc in each of next 2 sc. (*24 sc*)

Rnd 3: *[Sc in next sc, 2 sc in next sc] twice, sc in each of next 4 sc, [2 sc in next sc, sc in next sc] twice, rep from * once. (*32 sc*)

Rnd 4: [Sc in each of next 3 sc, 2 sc in next sc] 8 times. (*40 sc*)

Rnd 5: Working in **back lps** (*see Stitch Guide*) only, sc in each sc around, join in first sc. Fasten off.

Rnd 6: Join white with sc in first sc, sc in each rem sc around.

Rnds 7 & 8: Sc in each sc around.

Rnd 9: Sc in each of next 12 sc, [sc dec in next 2 sc] 8 times, sc in each of next 12 sc. (*32 sc*)

Rnd 10: Sc in each of next 10 sc, [sc dec in next 2 sc] 6 times, sc in each of next 10 sc. (*26 sc*)

Rnds 11–14: Sc in each sc around.

Rnd 15: Sc in each of next 6 sc, 2 sc in next sc, sc in each of next 12 sc, 2 sc in next sc, sc in each of next 6 sc. (*28 sc*)

Rnd 16: Sc in each of next 7 sc, 2 sc in next sc, sc in each of next 12 sc, 2 sc in next sc, sc in each of next 7 sc. (*30 sc*)

Rnd 17: Sc in each of next 7 sc, 2 sc in next sc, sc in each of next 14 sc, 2 sc in next sc, sc in each of next 7 sc. (*32 sc*)

Rnd 18: Sc in each of next 8 sc, 2 sc in next sc, sc in each of next 14 sc, 2 sc in next sc, sc in each of next 8 sc. (*34 sc*)

Rnd 19: Sc in each of next 8 sc, 2 sc in next sc, sc in each of next 16 sc, 2 sc in next sc, sc in each of next 8 sc, join in first sc. Leaving an 18-inch end for sewing, fasten off. (*36 sc*)

Stuff firmly. Sew Legs to sides of Body about 2½ inches apart so Doorstop will be in a sitting position (*see photo*).

ARM

Make 2.

Rnd 1 (RS): With 2 strands of lavender, ch 3, join in first ch to form a ring, ch 1, 2 sc in each ch around. (*6 sc*)

Rnd 2: 2 sc in each sc around. (*12 sc*)

Rnd 3: [Sc in each of next 2 sc, 2 sc in next sc] 4 times. (*16 sc*)

Rnd 4: [Sc in next sc, 2 sc in next sc] 8 times. (*24 sc*)

Rnd 5: Working in back lps only, sc in each sc around, join in first sc. Fasten off.

Rnd 6: Join white with sc in first sc, sc in each rem sc around.

Rnds 7–20: Sc in each sc around.

Rnd 21: Sc in each sc around, join in first sc. Leaving an 18-inch end for sewing, fasten off.

Stuff firmly. Flatten top of Arm and sew closed. Sew 1 Arm to each side of Body beg 2 rnds below where Head and Body are joined.

MUZZLE

Rnd 1 (RS): With 2 strands of white, ch 3, join in first ch to form a ring, ch 1, 2 sc in each ch around. (*6 sc*)

Rnd 2: 2 sc in each sc around. (*12 sc*)

Rnd 3: 2 sc in each sc around. (*24 sc*)

Rnds 4–9: Sc in each sc around.

Rnd 10: [Sc in each of next 3 sc, 2 sc in next sc] 6 times. (*30 sc*)

Rnds 11 & 12: Sc in each sc around.

Rnd 13: [Sc in each of next 4 sc, 2 sc in next sc] 6 times. *(36 sc)*

Rnd 14: Sc in each sc around.

Rnd 15: Sc in each sc around, join in first sc. Fasten off.

Stuff lightly. Sew to front of Head over rnds 13–24.

HORN
Rnd 1 (RS): With 2 strands of lavender, ch 2, 4 sc in back lp of 2nd ch from hook. *(4 sc)*

Note: Work following rnds in back lps only unless otherwise stated.

Rnd 2: [Sc in next sc, 2 sc in next sc] twice. *(6 sc)*

Rnd 3: Sc in each sc around.

Rnd 4: [Sc in each of next 2 sc, 2 sc in next sc] twice. *(8 sc)*

Rnd 5: Rep rnd 3.

Rnd 6: [Sc in each of next 3 sc, 2 sc in next sc] twice. *(10 sc)*

Rnd 7: Rep rnd 3.

Rnd 8: [Sc in each of next 4 sc, 2 sc in next sc] twice. *(12 sc)*

Rnd 9: Rep rnd 3.

Rnd 10: [Sc in each of next 5 sc, 2 sc in next sc] twice. *(14 sc)*

Rnd 11: Rep rnd 3.

Rnd 12: [Sc in each of next 6 sc, 2 sc in next sc] twice. *(16 sc)*

Rnd 13: Sc in each sc around, join in beg sc. Leaving a 12-inch end for sewing, fasten off.

Sew to top of Head, slightly forward of center.

EAR
Make 2.
Rnd 1 (RS): With 2 strands of white, ch 3, join in first ch to form a ring, ch 1, 2 sc in each ch around. *(6 sc)*

Rnd 2: [Sc in each of next 2 sc, 2 sc in next sc] twice. *(8 sc)*

Rnd 3: [Sc in each of next 3 sc, 2 sc in next sc] twice. *(10 sc)*

Rnd 4: [Sc in each of next 4 sc, 2 sc in next sc] twice. *(12 sc)*

Rnd 5: Sc in each sc around, join in beg sc. Leaving a 12-inch end for sewing, fasten off.

Flatten each Ear. Sew to Head on each side of Horn.

MANE
For each fringe, cut 4 strands of white, each 18 inches long. With all 4 strands held tog, fold in half, insert hook around st, draw fold through st, draw all loose ends through fold. Tighten.

Starting at top of Head behind Horn, work fringe in each st across back of Head down to neck in a point. Work 3 rows of fringe across front of Head below Horn. Trim fringe in front of Head to about 2 inches. Trim Mane as desired.

TAIL
Cut 80 strands of white, each 18 inches long. Tie 2 separate strands of white tightly around middle of strands. Tie to center back of Body over rnd 17.

FINISHING
Step 1: Glue rickrack around rnd 5 of each Arm. Rep on rnd 5 of each Leg.

Step 2: Starting at rnd 1 of Horn, wrap rickrack around each rnd continuously to last rnd, securing with glue as you go.

Step 3: Tie wire-edged ribbon in bow around neck.

Step 4: Glue ribbon roses at random over Mane.

Step 5: For eyes, cut pieces from felt according to pattern pieces. With pupil set downward, glue to front of eye white, glue back of eye white to eye back. Glue to Head and last rnd of Muzzle about 1½ inches apart.

Step 6: For nostrils, cut pieces from black felt according to diagram piece *(see Nostril Diagram)*. Glue to inside of each Nostril. ■

Pupil
Cut 2 from
black felt.

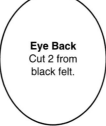

Eye White
Cut 2 from
white felt.

Eye Back
Cut 2 from
black felt.

Unicorn Doorstop
Nostril Diagram
Cut 2 from black felt.

Annie's Attic®

TOLL-FREE ORDER LINE or to request a free catalog (800) LV-ANNIE (800) 582-6643
Customer Service (800) AT-ANNIE (800) 282-6643, **Fax** (800) 882-6643
Visit anniesattic.com

We have made every effort to ensure the accuracy and completeness of these instructions.
We cannot, however, be responsible for human error, typographical mistakes or variations in individual work.

ISBN: 978-1-59635-222-3

Stitch Guide

For more complete information, visit **FreePatterns.com**

ABBREVIATIONS

beg	begin/begins/beginning
bpdc	back post double crochet
bpsc	back post single crochet
bptr	back post treble crochet
CC	contrasting color
ch(s)	chain(s)
ch-	refers to chain or space previously made (i.e. ch-1 space)
ch sp(s)	chain space(s)
cl(s)	cluster(s)
cm	centimeter(s)
dc	double crochet (singular/plural)
dc dec	double crochet 2 or more stitches together, as indicated
dec	decrease/decreases/decreasing
dtr	double treble crochet
ext	extended
fpdc	front post double crochet
fpsc	front post single crochet
fptr	front post treble crochet
g	gram(s)
hdc	half double crochet
hdc dec	half double crochet 2 or more stitches together, as indicated
inc	increase/increases/increasing
lp(s)	loop(s)
MC	main color
mm	millimeter(s)
oz	ounce(s)
pc	popcorn(s)
rem	remain/remains/remaining
rep(s)	repeat(s)
rnd(s)	round(s)
RS	right side
sc	single crochet (singular/plural)
sc dec	single crochet 2 or more stitches together, as indicated
sk	skip/skipped/skipping
sl st(s)	slip stitch(es)
sp(s)	space(s)/spaced
st(s)	stitch(es)
tog	together
tr	treble crochet
trtr	triple treble
WS	wrong side
yd(s)	yard(s)
yo	yarn over

Chain—ch: Yo, pull through lp on hook.

Slip stitch—sl st: Insert hook in st, pull through both lps on hook.

Single crochet—sc: Insert hook in st, yo, pull through st, yo, pull through both lps on hook.

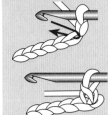

Front post stitch—fp: Back post stitch—bp: When working post st, insert hook from right to left around post st on previous row.

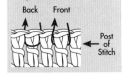

Front loop—front lp Back loop—back lp

Front Loop   Back Loop

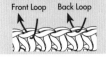

Half double crochet— hdc: Yo, insert hook in st, yo, pull through st, yo, pull through all 3 lps on hook.

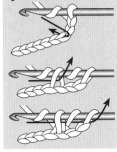

Double crochet—dc: Yo, insert hook in st, yo, pull through st, [yo, pull through 2 lps] twice.

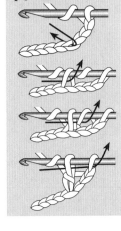

Change colors: Drop first color; with 2nd color, pull through last 2 lps of st.

Treble crochet—tr: Yo twice, insert hook in st, yo, pull through st, [yo, pull through 2 lps] 3 times.

Double treble crochet—dtr: Yo 3 times, insert hook in st, yo, pull through st, [yo, pull through 2 lps] 4 times.

Single crochet decrease (sc dec): (Insert hook, yo, draw lp through) in each of the sts indicated, yo, draw through all lps on hook.

Example of 2-sc dec

Half double crochet decrease (hdc dec): (Yo, insert hook, yo, draw lp through) in each of the sts indicated, yo, draw through all lps on hook.

Example of 2-hdc dec

Double crochet decrease (dc dec): (Yo, insert hook, yo, draw loop through, draw through 2 lps on hook) in each of the sts indicated, yo, draw through all lps on hook.

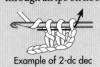

Example of 2-dc dec

Treble crochet decrease (tr dec): Holding back last lp of each st, tr in each of the sts indicated, yo, pull through all lps on hook.

Example of 2-tr dec

US		UK
sl st (slip stitch)	=	sc (single crochet)
sc (single crochet)	=	dc (double crochet)
hdc (half double crochet)	=	htr (half treble crochet)
dc (double crochet)	=	tr (treble crochet)
tr (treble crochet)	=	dtr (double treble crochet)
dtr (double treble crochet)	=	ttr (triple treble crochet)
skip	=	miss